THE DRAGONS,
THE GIANT, THE WOMEN

ALSO BY WAYÉTU MOORE

She Would Be King

THE DRAGONS, THE GIANT, THE WOMEN

A MEMOIR

WAYÉTU MOORE

GRAYWOLF PRESS

This publication is made possible, in part, by the voters of Minnesota through a Minnesota State Arts Board Operating Support grant, thanks to a legislative appropriation from the arts and cultural heritage fund. Significant support has also been provided by Target, the McKnight Foundation, the Lannan Foundation, the Amazon Literary Partnership, and other generous contributions from foundations, corporations, and individuals. To these organizations and individuals we offer our heartfelt thanks.

Published by Graywolf Press
250 Third Avenue North, Suite 600
Minneapolis, Minnesota 55401

www.graywolfpress.org

Published in the United States of America

ISBN 978-1-64445-031-4

2 4 6 8 9 7 5 3 1
First Graywolf Printing, 2020

Library of Congress Control Number: 2019949911

Jacket design: Kimberly Glyder

Jacket art: Shutterstock

For Junior & David.

Whatever you are, I am.

Take your broken heart, make it into art.

—CARRIE FISHER

AUTHOR'S NOTE

I have tried to recreate events, locales, and conversations from my memories of them. In order to maintain their anonymity, in some instances I have changed the names of individuals and places, and I may have changed some identifying characteristics and details such as physical properties, occupations, and places of residence.

THE DRAGONS,
THE GIANT, THE WOMEN

RAINY
SEASON

ONE

Mam. I heard it again from another room, as I always did when the adults were careful not to mention her name around me, as if it was both a sacred thing and cause for punishment, and I ran toward it. Mam is what they called her then. Down hallways, across the yard, behind closed doors—her name the most timid kind of ghost. "Mam so beautiful" or "Mam used to go there plenty" or "That's not the way Mam cooked it" they would say quietly, cautious not to raise the drapes with the wind of their voices. And I would stumble in, wanting to catch them in the act, to give me that word again for so long that I fell asleep to the sound of it. Startled by my tiny body, they would stop and ask if I had finished my lessons or if I wanted a snack.

Once when it was raining, I heard her voice outside. An Ol' Ma, a grand-aunt maybe, told us that all of our dead and missing were resting peacefully in wandering clouds, and when it rains and you listen closely you can hear the things they forgot to tell you before leaving. Mam was not dead, they said, but I stumbled into the rain and stood beside the rosebush where I was sure I had heard her voice, full of laughter and long ago, singing those forgotten things.

"Tell me where she is," I would ask.

"In America, you girl. I told you. In New York," they would say.

"Are you sure?" I asked to be certain. "When will we see her again?"

"Soon," they said.

"Can I go there?" I asked, though I knew the answer.

"Why would you want to go there, you girl?"

They convinced me that Liberia's sweetness was incomparable—more than a ripe mango's strings hanging between my teeth after sucking the juice of every sticky bite, the Ol' Ma's milk candy that melted on my tongue, sugar bread, even America—none a match for the taste then, of my country. This was all I knew of my home then—that I lived in a place that made words sing, so sweet. Yet it was without my mother.

In those years, turning five years old tasted like Tang powder on the porch after supper. Little boys drove with their Ol' Pas, a grandfather or other old man with pupils eclipsed with a dwelling blue, to the Atlantic, to fish facing the sunset. Little boys sat in parlors of opaque tobacco smoke as they watched Oppong Weah kick soccer balls into checkered nets against Chelsea. Little boys could now walk alone to those junction markets that sold everything from bushmeat to shoestring, to buy the plantains and eggplant driven from Nimba's farms for their nagging Ol' Mas.

Little girls could now help to wash sinks of collard greens in front of kitchen windows that faced pepper gardens. Little girls could draw water from neighborhood wells and balance them on their heads, full of braids and restless musings, all the way back to their houses as the sun lingered at the edge of the sky to make sure they had safe walks home.

I turned five that day and the greens felt soft between my hands. They only let me wash them once, and afterward I was pushed away and told to leave the cooking to the cooks.

"You will have plenty time to wash greens, you girl," Korkor said, laughing from the hollow between the wide gap of her two front teeth.

"But I want to wash them longer," I said.

She picked me up from the stool in front of the sink and carried me to a table where a cake tempted me from the middle of snack plates.

"Look, you will spoil your fine dress!" she said, straightening the purple linen.

"The Ol' Pa will be vexed if you spoil your fine dress," she rambled, and returned to the sink to complete the cleansing and preparation of my birthday greens. I did not believe that my grandfather would be angry with me if I spilled water from the greens on the dress he had sewn for my birthday. No, Charles Freeman would be proud that he would have one more granddaughter whom he could send for water from the well in Logan Town where he lived with Ol' Ma.

It was a famous well, mentioned in many of Ol' Ma's stories about Mam's childhood and those memories of her life before us. It was better than the well near their old home further inside Logan Town. Ol' Pa was a tailor and Ol' Ma was a shop owner then, and they had moved with other Vai people toward the city, where most settled in Logan Town after a man they call Tubman, the president at the time, gave jobs to rural Liberians. It was 1966.

They say the water well was a ground-level brick structure with concrete lining similar to most wells in Logan Town. It was a hand-drawn well with a bucket that dropped quickly in and out. As the bucket rose, Mam would grab the handle and pull it toward her small body to empty the water into her own plastic bucket. Once, alone in the yard, Mam peeked over the well and sang into it, as they say she always did, and the well threw an echo back up. "Dance with me," she sang, and the well repeated her words, spitting a familiar voice onto the yard. She laughed, and while raising one of her hands to cover her mouth, Mam lost her balance and fell into the well. Darkness smothered her and the water below swallowed her body. The bucket rose and Mam spat the coldness out of her nose and mouth, gripped the rope, and yelled so that someone would hear her. As the bucket ascended, she heaved what she could out of her system and yelled again, scraping her fingers on the inside walls for something she could hold on to. The bucket fell again, and this time she did not know if she was moving or still, if the darkness was her end; the sunlight was so close and yet it mocked her in the distance. When the bucket resurfaced from the water, Mam's grip on the rope loosened, and when she opened her mouth to yell, nothing came out. She stretched out her hands, expecting to scrape the concrete walls, to fall again and be lost forever in the Logan Town shadows, but instead, as the bucket rose she felt a coarse palm wrap around her right wrist. Her head lay limp on her shoulder as her body was raised out of the well. It was a Ghanaian neighbor, Mr. Kofi, whom Mam was known to taunt through her window as he walked to work every day. "Thank you," Mam whimpered, barely conscious. From then on, Ol' Pa made sure he sent at least two daughters or granddaughters to the well.

I turned five that day so I knew that I could now be called to go too.

"But you say I can wash them today," I said, turning from the pink and yellow birthday fixtures on the table back to Korkor. "You say I can wash them."

"And I let you wash them, enneh-so?" she said, placing the greens into a bowl on the counter. Korkor wiped her hands on the lappa tied around her waist and came to me. She took my hand and led me to the den and I dragged my feet so that my white dress shoes scraped the floor behind her.

"Torma!" Korkor yelled out. "Torma, come get this girl."

In the den, Torma sat with my sisters, Wi and K, in front of a game of Chutes and Ladders.

"Come," Torma said, taking my fallen fingers. "Come play, small girl. Be on my team. I winning," she assured me.

Torma was a teenage Vai girl from the village of Lai, a third cousin, another caretaker who boarded with us after Mam left. Papa paid for Torma's education in Monrovia, and she, in turn, took care of my sisters and me in Mam's absence. Korkor mentioned once that the girls from Lai made good mothers. I cried the night she moved in and told Papa that I did not want anyone else to come be my "mama."

"She will not be your mama. Mam is coming back. She will be your friend." When Torma stepped out of Papa's pickup truck, she was introduced as "your cousin from Lai. Your big sister." She kept to herself mostly, and alongside Korkor if she was not at the table reading or "taking care of lesson." Over time the same orange shirt she was wearing on the day that I met her became faded and stained with spilled food. Finger paint remained splattered between the buttons, no matter how many times she washed it.

"Look, we winning," Torma said as I knelt in front of the board game. K, a three-year-old with a charming round face who knew the power of being the youngest of the three of us girls, parked in Torma's lap as soon as she sat back on the floor. She would turn four in only two months and looked to have been coerced to behaving with a party of her own. She twirled the barrette that stopped one of her pigtails between her fingers and smiled toward Wi, my six-year-old sister who concentrated on the board. The den was decorated with colorful helium balloons and metallic streamers taped neatly onto the folds where our walls met.

"Where my papa?" I asked Torma.

"Your papa outside with Moneysweet and Pastor," she said, and sucked her teeth as I bounded out of the room and onto the porch deck of our yard.

Papa sat in a deck chair beside the pastor of our church, a man who always gently shook my hand when he saw me. The reflection of their water glasses speckled the plastic table where they sat. It was a warm day, and the leaves of towering palm trees swayed above us amid a vast field of freshly watered grass. A radio rested on the rail of the deck and the exaggerated harmonies, the clashing of cymbals and drums, filled the surrounding yard. Papa's and Pastor's smiles bent to the rhythm as it vibrated the metal antennae. Moneysweet sat on a stool near the table and peeled a mango plum with a sharp knife. The sweat from his orange, square head descended both sides of his face in the sun, and upon seeing me he extended a slice of plum in my direction.

"Papa," I said, whining as I climbed into Papa's lap. "Korkor say I will wash greens on my birthday and then today she say not for long."

"You wash greens you will spoil your dress," he said, repeating Korkor's warning.

"I will not spoil it," I insisted.

"Wait, small small," he said. "After your party you will wash the greens."

I bit down on the ripe plum wedge, and the juice from it oozed out and followed the lines of my lips and jaw until the bottom of my face was completely sticky and wet. I worried that Papa would see me and send me back inside to Korkor or Torma to wipe my face, but he and Pastor had already resumed a conversation about a man whose name I heard at least once a day.

"But Doe has spoiled the country. Liberia spoiled-oh," Pastor said, shaking his head.

"It's not spoiled. Two more years the man's gone. A new president will come."

"He will rig the thing like he rigged the last one. Everybody fighting, everybody wants to be president. Everybody says they president," Pastor continued.

"Yeh, the country spoiled. Sam Doe spoiled it," Moneysweet agreed from the corner of the deck before shoving another slice of plum in his mouth.

I asked Ol' Ma who this man was, Samuel Doe, whose name I heard once a day, and she told me he was president of Liberia. Every time I listened to people talk about this man, it reminded me of the Hawa Undu dragon, the monster in my dreams, the sum of stories I was too young to hear. The Hawa Undu dragon was once a prince with good intentions, who entered the forest to avenge the death of his family, all buried now in the hills of Bomi County. He was a handsome prince, tall with broad shoulders, high cheeks, and coarse hands marked by the victory of his battles. He entered the forest and told the people that he would kill the dragons who left mountains of ashes in Buchanan and Virginia, who left poisoned eggs in Careysburg and Kakata. But the prince became a dragon himself. One with asymmetrical teeth, taloned elbows, and paper-thin eyes. One with a crooked back, coarse like the hollows of the iron mines where many sons were still lost, always dying. One rich enough to fly, yet too poor to know where to go. He humbugged the animals, killed for food, forgot his promises. And now, Hawa Undu was president of Liberia, once a prince with good intentions. Ol' Ma said everybody was talking about him because there was another prince who wanted to enter the forest and kill Hawa Undu, to restore peace. This prince was named Charles, like my Ol' Pa. Some thought he would be the real thing—that he could kill Hawa Undu and put an end to the haunting of the forest and the spirit princes who danced throughout—but others feared he would be the same, that no prince could enter the forest and keep his intentions. The woods will blind, will blunder. Hawa Undu would never die.

"You see the Burkina Faso rebels them have entered the country, and come start killing Krahn people left and right because Doe is Krahn man. You don't think they will kill Doe? They going for him," Pastor said, rubbing his chin.

"You hear from Patrick?" Papa asked after a moment.

"No, the people say he went and collected his Ol' Ma from the bush and went to Ghana," Pastor said.

"His house still there?"

"They looted it, I hear. But they didn't get much," Pastor continued.

"Mr. Patrick?" I asked. My father nodded, reluctantly. "Mr. Patrick is in Ghana?"

To this he did not respond, and I wondered about Mr. Patrick and Ms. Genevieve, his wife, and their two sons. Ms. Genevieve always gave us milk candy when we visited their house in Sinkor, which was so big that ten women were able to fit their markets in the front.

"All the Gio and Mano people running."

"Patrick was safe, my man. Doe's people were not looking for him. They know he was not giving money for no rebel business," Papa said.

"Doe's soldiers don't know nothing. They see Mano man, he gone."

"Hm. Everybody say they will kill man in power and lead better. Say they want kill Krahn man 'cause Krahn man not good president," Papa argued.

"And Krahn man want kill Gio man and Mano man," Moneysweet added. "For what?"

"And Gio man want kill Mandingo man," Pastor said loudly as he pointed at Moneysweet.

"And every man want kill Congo man," Papa said, almost singing. "Quiwonpka tried and now the man dead, enneh-so?"

Moneysweet laughed, wiped his sticky hands on his jeans, and stood up from the stool where he sat, shaking his head. He vanished into the house and reemerged with a napkin that he used to wipe my face.

"You will leave, Mr. Moore?" Moneysweet asked Papa.

When I asked my teacher what happened to Kelly, what happened to Josephine, what happened to Wiatta, what happened to Gerald, what happened to Saa, she murmured, America. I did not believe her until I stopped seeing them. I did not have a chance to share what I wanted to tell Mam in case they saw her.

"No. Me, I'm staying. The people are not serious," Papa said. "When the people realize it's a waste of time trying to push the man out and let him just go on his own through the next election, the country will go back to normal."

"Hmph. He will not go on his own-oh. He will not go," Pastor said matter-of-factly.

Through a green and clear Liberian April, a car approached us from the flat road with shoulders and elbows sticking out of its windows. When it parked in front of the deck, I stood up when I recognized Mam's parents, my Ol' Ma and Ol' Pa, whom we called Ma and Pa. My uncle was with them also, and a cousin and his mother. I stood up from where I sat with Papa and ran to Pa, a towering man with a round bald head, whose face I could barely see when I looked up and the sun was its highest.

"Birthday geh," he said, picking me up with great difficulty as soon as he stepped out of the car.

"Look, my dress," I said into his face.

"It looks good," Ma said, touching the lace cloth that lined the hem.

My sisters, who heard their voices from inside, bolted toward Ma and Pa, nearly bowling them over with the charge.

The men settled on the porch with Papa and Pastor. They were mostly dark and stout men who all appeared serious, only to collectively descend into an abyss of laughter at the right word or joke at an unfortunate person's expense. Korkor walked onto the deck and told the guests that the food was ready, then she whispered something into Ol' Ma's ear. Beyond the den and around the dining room table, my family was gathered behind a cake with burning candles coming from its face. They noticed me and began to clap and holler, and Ol' Ma pushed me toward the table and cake from behind. It became quiet and I was sure they would all sing.

"Where is Mam?" K asked.

Mam. It remained silent for a moment. It was a moment like a box packed tight and closed for so long that when it was finally opened its contents rushed out. I did not wait for them to bellow the birthday song, but ran into my room and stared out of the window. Mam. Korkor came behind me, and Papa, but none would pull me away. Not the smell of fresh greens, not my Ol' Ma, not my Ol' Pa. Not the cake and streamers, or turning five. I remained near the window waiting. I needed it to rain again. I wanted to hear Mam sing.

TWO

In the months after Mam left Liberia for New York, we talked to her every Sunday. She sounded the same to me then, though once or twice her voice disappeared while she spoke. I inhaled the heavy silence, hoping that some of her would seep through the phone so that I could lay my head against it.

"I will soon be back, yeh?" she would say.

After moving into the house with palm trees, I found that her smell had moved with us, followed me as I, on so many Saturday afternoons, had trailed her around the apartment in her red high heels that dragged underneath my feet. In her closet, in her room, in the kitchen, even Korkor smelled like her—the calming blend of seasoned greens and rose water.

Every day our driver, a short, chubby man with a blunt line of gray hair an inch above each ear, picked us up from school. Torma met him at the end of the road to walk us home. From the main road we could see our house dancing in the heated rays of the sun, a drawing that grew bigger and more real with each step. We stumbled out of the car in uniform plaid skirts and small pink backpacks. Torma waved at our driver as his tires blew a whirl of dust into the air when he drove away.

"Come," Torma said, turning around to us. "Surprise for you all inside."

Upon hearing the word, we sprinted down the dusty road. It was dry season in Monrovia and the sun strained its eyes, burning arms and feet as we ran. Moneysweet waved from a rosebush in the front yard and we waved back before nearly tripping over our feet into the house.

"Surprise today," he said as we climbed, one step at a time, up the porch stairs. He laughed and shook his head at our excitement.

Inside, there was no father or grandparents. The foyer was empty. We searched our rooms and found nothing of importance or shock, so we approached Torma in the hallway.

"You girls fast," she said.

"Where's the surprise?" Wi asked.

"In the den," Torma said. Before she finished the sentence, we were in full stride through the front hallway toward the den.

In the den, near my mother's scented couch, there was a large brown envelope with black writing and stickers on it. Anytime something like this sat on the table when we came home, it meant that Mam had sent something for us.

"It's from New York! It's from New York!" we chanted and took turns waving the large envelope in the air.

The front door opened and after a short set of footsteps, Papa walked into the den.

"Mr. Moore, you here?" Torma asked, quickly standing. He motioned for her to sit down and allowed us to jump around the room before throwing our arms around his neck.

"I got in early. It came, enneh-so?" Papa asked. Torma nodded. She walked out of the den and returned with a pair of scissors. She cut the tape on the envelope and opened it. I reached inside.

"What is this?" I asked disappointedly. Two small boxes that looked like video cases lay inside the box with a letter.

"Movies," Papa said as K pinched his cheeks, already distracted by his presence from the mysterious box that she was shouting over only a few seconds earlier.

"Ma-Ma-lawa?" K asked in his lap.

"No, not that movie," he said. The Malawala Balawala country dancers were K's favorite. The people on the two boxes I held looked different. On one box there was a girl with white skin and a blue dress, a little dog, and three Gio devils that were connected at their hips. The other was a woman with white skin and white hair with her hands stretched out in grass. I was confused.

"Read it," Papa said.

"*Wiz-ard of Oz,*" Wi read from the box with the Gio devils.

"*Sound of Mu-sic,*" she read from the other box.

I was still confused.

"Why do they look like that?" I asked.

"Like what?" Papa asked.

"Like, sick. White, an—" I said.

"They don't look sick. They just have different color skin. Like the missionary woman, Sis' Walton," Papa said.

"What?" I asked, disappointed.

"Like our neighbors," he said.

"The neighbor not white," I said.

"No," Papa continued. "But he is different color."

Torma held her hand to her mouth and giggled.

Papa stood up and took the movie from my hand. He put it in the VCR and turned on the television. He stood for a while in front of the television and then walked behind it and fidgeted with a long black cord.

"This cord is spoiled. Who spoiled the cord?" he asked, lifting the stretch of cord where tiny red and green wires peeked distortedly out of their leather shield. I would have suggested that it was K and her incessant viewing of the Malawala Balawala country dancers, but I knew Papa would call it "frisky" and I did not want to risk watching the white people.

"Mr. Moore, I can go to the store," Torma suggested.

Papa shook his head as Moneysweet walked through the den door.

"Mr. Moore, I'm finished," Moneysweet said, still sweating.

"Moneysweet, you can go to the market for VCR cord?" he asked.

"Sorry, Mr. Moore, I'm meeting friends tonight," he said.

Papa nodded and reached his hands into his pocket. He paid Moneysweet his daily wages, and Moneysweet walked through the den to his garage apartment.

"Have fun with your surprise," he said, walking out.

Papa folded his hands.

"I know. Let's go see if the neighbor has a cord," he said.

Wi and K jumped out of their seats. I was not so quick to move. This news of our neighbor's possible "whiteness" both frightened and angered me.

Our neighbors lived behind a tall cement wall crowned with barbed wire. Papa said they blocked off their house like this because the rogues kept coming to steal from them. Their gate was open, so we walked through. When he opened his door, I did not know what to expect. I thought he would be as blue as my skirt or as orange as Torma's shirt. He was, however, still the same as the last time I saw him.

"Hello, Mr. Moore, girls," he said, nodding toward us with his syrupy accent. They said hello. I whispered it while inspecting his face for rainbows.

"Hello," Papa said. "The girls and I wanted to know if you had an extra VCR cord. Mam sent a video from America that they want to watch," he said.

"Sure, sure, yes," our neighbor said and invited us into his house. Their den was decorated with porcelain statues and many pictures of their lives and family in China. Bright red drapes hung down to the floor and the gray couches and chairs were covered with plastic. His wife came toward us from the back of their house. She shook Papa's hand and nodded her entire body toward him multiple times. Our neighbor returned to the room with the cord, and after taking it from him, Papa became distracted by a stack of boxes in the corner. He fidgeted with the cord and stared at the boxes, then at our neighbor in concern.

"You planning to move?" he asked, pointing toward the boxes.

Our neighbor put his arm around his wife's shoulder, squeezing it underneath his fingers.

"Yes, yes, we going back for a while," he said, and glanced at my sisters and me.

"Why? What about your business?"

Our neighbor removed his arm from around his wife's shoulder.

"Mr. Moore, can I talk to you? In the sitting room?" he asked. Papa nodded and followed, closing the door behind them.

"Wait here," his wife said with a voice as soft as feathers. She exited the den and my sisters and I were left standing alone. Behind the door, I heard Papa say Hawa Undu's name. He did not sound angry, but he was not laughing or smiling. I could tell he and our neighbor were very serious. There were many boxes in the corner. Torma said once that if someone came to remove Hawa Undu the dragon and the people started to fight, they would hurt not only other Liberians but also the Chinese people who were bad to them. And they would go find the Lebanese people, too, and they would hurt the boss man who slapped their sons at work. And they would find the professors who failed them for not being smart, the professors who did not take money for grades. And they would find the people who were rude to them once or twice, and those who had offended them years ago, and they would hurt them.

His wife returned to the room with three pieces of candy, which she gave to us, smiling. Shortly after, Papa and our neighbor came back.

"You should come too. Come with us to China," he joked, patting Papa's arm.

"No, no. We're staying here," Papa said. "Things will be fine. You will see."

"Yes, well. Hopefully. Then we come back," our neighbor laughed.

On the walk home I asked Papa what they had talked about in the room, but his eyes looked as serious as he sounded behind those doors. His grip on my hand was tighter than it was when we walked to our neighbor's house. He was murmuring to himself and he shook his head, as if he did not hear me, and he was sweating, because of the sun and maybe because of what they had talked about. I asked once more but a gust of wind upstaged me. Rainy season was coming and the wind was angrier every day.

The Sound of Music was the first film in. After the first several minutes of the movie, when I realized that none of them were going to turn purple, I learned about children like me, whose mother was far away. I wondered if Mam had seen this film and if she was singing along with me. When she called that Sunday and it was my turn to speak to her, I sang her the verses that I had memorized and she laughed on the other end of the phone.

"You learned the songs already?" she asked.

I agreed and sang, and as Mam joined me her voice left the small circle near my ear and filled our den with a soft alto trembling that could only be hers. When I forgot the words of the song, Mam continued until her voice broke on the other end of the phone.

"You there?" she asked.

"Yeh, Mama," I said, wanting all of her back in Liberia, hating the sound of music so far away.

Some Saturdays later, my Ol' Ma was visiting from her house in Logan Town and after eating breakfast, I led her to the den to watch *The Sound of Music* with me. I sang along, echoing their words since I did not know them, trailing behind a story that I could not fully understand. Wi and K sat in the den also. They were more entertained by the head tie wrapped around Ma's head than by the movie. They were taking turns unfolding it from her head and wrapping it around again.

There was a loud knocking at the front door that escalated to a persistent thud. Papa walked into the den from his room, and he looked like he was ready to yell at us for jumping or tapping on the walls.

"What's that sound?" he asked.

The thud was accompanied by a soft wailing, voices that at first sounded like singing, then rose to collective screams.

We turned toward the noise and the clamor of voices when a neighbor beat on the den window.

"Turn that down," Papa said, pointing toward the television while he opened the window.

"Mr. Moore! Mr. Moore!" The woman was Mam's friend, and she lived several houses past our neighbors. "They coming! The war now come! They coming!" she shouted.

"The rebels, most of them at the bridge now. Go, Mr. Moore! You all hurry and go!" she shouted and pointed in the direction of the Caldwell Bridge, only a quarter of a mile away from our house. As soon as the words left her mouth, she turned her head toward the sound down the road and ran at full speed toward a car that overflowed with clothes and disarrayed dishes and furniture. Her husband's hand beat the driver's door.

"Let's go!" he yelled to his wife as she jumped into the car and closed the door. He waved at Papa and the car sped off, followed by a cloud of dust.

Papa's eyes grew wide and he closed the window quickly. Torma and Korkor ran into the den.

"You all hear that noise? What's that noise?" Korkor asked hysterically. I turned away from the film and wondered why Torma looked afraid.

"Go get your shoes," Ma said to us.

"No, stay together," Papa said, holding out his hand.

"Hawa Un-" I tried to say.

"Shhh!" Papa said. "Y'all lie on the ground."

"Why?" Wi asked.

"We don't want them to see us," he said.

"Who?"

"Just stay here." Papa got to his knees and crawled across the den toward the hallway to his bedroom. When he reached the doorway, Korkor grabbed his arm from the floor.

"Mr. Moore. The war now come. My family," she said. She was crying now, shaking as sweat dampened her head tie.

Papa nodded and touched her hand.

"Go from the back. Hurry," he said. Korkor crawled out of the den and got up, running past the kitchen and out of the house, crying loudly as her head tie fell from her head and lay stranded on the tiles of our hallway.

Ma unraveled her head tie and used it to shield our bodies.

"Hide and seek?" K asked. Ma nodded, though her eyes looked less and less like Mam's as we lay there. "You all right, my children?" she whispered beneath the lappa. We nodded.

"It's the dragon?" I whispered and my Ol' Ma's face froze, as if recalling our stories, blackened and still.

Papa rushed back into the den with a backpack and three pairs of slippers.

"Crawl to the kitchen," he said, at first squatting, then he picked up K. Ma led us on our knees out of the den. When we reached the kitchen, Papa stood up and lifted us to our feet.

"Put these on," he demanded.

We put on the slippers as the popping sound got closer.

"Let's go!" Papa said, putting on the backpack as he raised K to his waist.

Ma picked me up and I watched Maria sing on the television screen until she was out of sight. We left the house from the back door, where Moneysweet was kneeled down peeking around the side of the house. Papa saw him and went to him, kneeling beside him.

"Come," Papa said to him, "we going through the woods."

Moneysweet hesitated.

"Mr. Moore, I can't go. I can't leave," he said.

Without asking, Papa hugged him. There was a back street to the highway behind a house across the road. Moneysweet squinted to get a clear view of it from where he knelt. He stood up with Papa and leaned against the back of the house, periodically looking out onto the road. He took several deep breaths, took Papa's hand and squeezed it, and ran across the yard. His shirt soared in the air as he sprinted from the back of the house, across the road to the street and highway.

"Where is Moneysweet going?" K asked softly.

"To visit his family."

"Why is he running?" I asked.

"Why not? Don't you like running? When I say go, we run," Papa said as soon as he saw Moneysweet disappear behind the house across the street. Ma put me down.

"You hear? When I say go, we run to the woods, okay?"

I waited while in the background "Edelweiss" was being sung by the captain and his eldest daughter in harmony. I smiled at my father.

"What is that sound?"

"Don't worry," Papa hurried to say. "When I say run, we run like Moneysweet."

Papa adjusted the straps of the backpack and the popping grew louder, and so close it sounded like the roses in Mam's bush were exploding at the other end of the house.

"Go!" Papa yelled.

We ran past the garage apartment through the mammoth yard as the popping in the air increased above us. I was not running fast enough and Papa pushed my back, his backpack flapping behind him. I swung my arms as hard as I could, and Torma pulled my hands until my legs ached, and I concentrated on the woods ahead.

"Go, go, go," he said. "Don't look behind." We ran through the yard away from the box and triangle and towering palm trees that we once drew. I was almost out of breath and I noticed Wi's slippers fall off her feet and stay behind in the thick grass. Papa went back to grab them, and we continued with Ma as the popping seemed to be coming from the leaves ahead. We reached the edge of the woods and ran until dense bushes that sat among the vast spread of trees covered us, and we could finally stop.

"Nah-mah. It's okay," Ma said, as we all panted together.

"Keep walking," Papa said, also out of breath. He picked up K and me, one on each hip, and continued to stride through the woods.

"Where we going now?" I asked, now uncertain of what game we were playing. I thought we would run to the woods, then back to the house. Ma stood up straight, heaving as she held Wi's hand. Torma trailed behind and the orange shirt she wore collected leaves and masses of sweat as we walked.

I stared at Papa and Ma rushing through the woods. They could not hear it, but it was there, whistling in the distance, just as I imagined from Ol' Ma's stories. Settled wings. They had come. A prince entered that distant forest to kill Hawa Undu. The war had just begun.

THREE

Bendu Sudan was not in the woods but she was the first face that I looked for after we entered. She scared me when I saw her on our television one night, her black face covered with clods of powder, screaming out to us from the screen. Papa said it was a foolish movie and that Bendu Sudan was just acting. But when she screamed she cried, her dress hanging off one shoulder, and it made me cry. At school some of the children said that she hides in the woods and the forests, and if you walk too far inside, she will grab you. So when we entered the woods after Ol' Ma and Papa pulled us out of the house, Bendu Sudan was the first person I looked for.

Bendu Sudan used to kiss a man who was married to another woman, a "big big" man, they say, with plenty money. And because she used to kiss him, and leave her lips pressed against his for a long time, and even sometimes use her tongue, even though he already had a wife, she was not a good woman. Her stomach started to get big because she was going to have his baby, and the big big man was afraid and angry because he did not want to tell his wife, so he killed Bendu Sudan. Bendu's Ol' Ma told her that when a person whose enemies have not been punished dies, that person could return to punish the enemies.

"Death is not the end of life for you" is what they said. Death is not the end. So after Bendu Sudan was gone, people would see her on the beach and around Monrovia, still a fine geh like when she was with the big big man. And if a married man ever tried to kiss her like the big big man did, she would haunt him. And she was so disappointed with the world that she would haunt others. So I searched the shadows of the trees around me for Bendu Sudan's face. And since death was not the end, I looked for others who may have gone some time ago, who were waiting in those shadowy places to correct their enemies. I looked up at the sky, without sun, without moon or clouds or stars, but Bendu was not there. If I were not so close to Papa, I was sure the ghost would leap out from the leaves to wrap her snakelike fingers around my neck. I had been at the edge of those woods many times before, but Torma or Korkor always stopped me from going farther. The woods were not for small small girls, they would say. There were some good things there, like almond trees and a looming plum tree Moneysweet picked from during the dry season, and we would wait at the edge of those mazes for what felt like an entire afternoon until he reemerged with a netted basket full of juicy red and orange plums, each as big as two fists. But we had heard stories of the badness of the woods too. Like Bendu Sudan. Like the dragons, smaller than Hawa Undu, scaly green creatures with sharklike teeth that even the bushmeat hunters were afraid to challenge. Like the boogeyman and devils. Like the Monkey Men who they say were made by scientists from America and Europe, to see if monkeys and people could fall in love, and were set free in the jungle to live in the mental wasteland of being half monkey and half people way too poor, too joyless to be rescued from surrendering their dignity. Like the children my aunty said work all day in the woods in Harbel tapping tapping tapping the Firestone trees until rubber snailed its way out to be packed in ships and sent to America—these children with no smiles, no stories of yesterday to tell, who had not eaten for so long that she once drove by Harbel and could not tell if they were still children or still people at all. All these things I had heard of these woods, and now the woods were all around me—whispering to us at first, then laughing as the birds slapped the tree branches above our heads in hurried flight. There was a sound like a first raindrop hitting an empty bucket, the hardest rain, loud and too many drops to count. And a sound like thunder, in the kind of storm that the clouds send when they are jealous of those below.

"What is that?" I asked Papa, the popping still around us. We were walking so quickly and his skin was wet with sweat. He moved branches out of the way so that Ol' Ma's path would be clear. He moved branches that made the faces of grieving men.

"Drums," Papa said. "That's a drum." And Torma and Ol' Ma glanced at him, then looked away, and I felt like I had learned something I was not supposed to know, like that the drums were secret or magic.

"I hear another one," K said and Papa was shaking as we ran. In the distance we heard yelling each time we heard the drum, and the air became smokey, as if something was burning on the stove, and cars were honking, and in the distance people were shouting and the sound of those drums came nearer.

"That's Malawala Balawala?" K asked, sobered a bit by the thought of festival dancers celebrating not too far away.

"Yes," Papa said, panting heavily. "Gbessie Kiazolu is dancing to the drums with the Malawala Balawala country dancers."

"There's another!" K shouted. I heard it too. It was so loud that I felt the sound behind my eyes. People were running on the road when we left our house, not just us, but it felt like we were alone. Papa and Ol' Ma, Torma and my sisters and me. I missed Mam and if we did not go back to our house, we could not see her if she came back. So I cried.

"Sh, sh," Papa said, tapping my leg.

"The people will hear us-oh," Torma warned.

"What people?" Wi asked, turning to face Torma.

"The bad people," she answered.

"Sh, sh," Papa said. "You don't want go see Malawala Balawala? Want to go dance?"

I looked behind his shoulder. The color of the house was first to disappear through the leaves, then the shape, then the hammock that swung between two posts on the back porch. Sun-dried leaves and sticks cracked beneath Papa's shoes.

"Where is Mam?" Wi asked.

"We are going to her. We will see her soon, yeh?" Papa said, and he smiled as we worked our way through the branches, the drumming all around us. This made me more happy than I expected to feel. We would see Mam soon.

"But how will she know we left the house? She will wait there?" I asked.

"Just walk quick quick," he said, at first too fast. "She will know," he said, slower this time, and smiled. I clenched his shirt between my palms as the drums escalated. I wondered who was dancing on the other side, and if we would be allowed to sit with Papa and Ol' Ma or if we would have to dance with other children. Who would I see there? If this was all for Hawa Undu, then he certainly was a mighty dragon— one who needed thunder and drums to announce his battles.

"Gus, the people will enter the woods? They saw us?" my Ol' Ma asked. Her voice shook as she lifted Wi up so that her legs dangled over a large tree stump.

"No. I don't think so. Just keep going," Papa answered, moving even quicker.

"I tired, Mr. Moore," Torma gasped behind us.

"No, no. We can't stop," he said. "Pastor house will be right there on the other side."

"We going to Pastor house to dance?' I asked.

"Yes, that's where we going."

A willowy stream of sunlight bled through the high branches and rested on the side of his face.

"Papa," I whispered into the light.

"The man now come make his trouble everybody trouble," Ol' Ma murmured, louder than me so Papa did not hear me.

"Ma, we will be fine. Pastor house coming. Just pray," Papa assured her.

"No, that Charles Taylor trouble here," Torma said between heavy breaths behind us. "He want be president, that's not the way to do it. Go find boys and give them guns to fight your war? Now look."

The man she spoke of was the prince. He was the prince who had come to kill Hawa Undu. In their stories, the prince was born in Liberia but he moved to America after stealing from Hawa Undu. He came back with boys from Burkina Faso and Guinea, the rebels, and now he would force the dragon out of the forest.

"The monsters came for the dragon?" I asked, and Papa and Ol' Ma glanced at each other again in that language that only the old ones spoke, and they agreed.

"Torma, come!" Papa said, turning around as he noticed she had stopped to lean against a tree and catch her breath. She continued behind Papa, scratching her exposed legs as bristly weeds rubbed against them.

"We have to find phone to call Ol' Pa in Logan Town," Ol' Ma continued, pulling her lappa over her knees as she stepped over a large branch, the colors paled and ruined. I thought the woods would come alive with every mystical creature that had ever scared me as I walked behind Papa, the breaking leaves underneath his shoes, the heavy breathing and the splitting of the afternoon light.

"Papa, I'm scared," I said and he finally heard me.

"Nah-mah. We will be out here soon, yeh?" he said.

"Then we will go to Mam?"

He sounded as though he was about to say something else, but before the words could leave his mouth a loud crack made us stop.

"Down!" Papa said, kneeling. Torma ducked to the ground and covered her head. Ol' Ma leaned against a large tree with Wi's head pressed against her stomach. She was shaking as she looked back at the path that led us away from the house.

"Gus! Look!" she shouted, pointing to the trunk of the tree that she thought would protect her. Up from the buttress, a slowly rising vapor of smoke ascended from a dark hole where Wi, just a few moments before, was standing, and Ma once again broke with tears.

"They shooting in the woods," she said.

"Shooting what?" I asked. "What is shooting?"

"No, not in the woods," Papa said, standing up from where he knelt. "No shooting. I told you, drums—"

And before he could finish what he was saying, those drums came crashing loudly around us. "Let's go!" he shouted and ran between the trees as K and my head bobbed over his shoulders and by his side. Torma's arms swung beside her as she followed, and the cracks fell onto us and the surrounding woods.

"Run!" Papa said, and Ol' Ma led Wi across the uprooted stems as the trees around me came alive. Up from the darkest greens and roaring howls, square faces and sharp teeth appeared in the crevasses of the branches. The boogeyman and Bendu Sudan, Monkey Men and Firestone's children with scowls so convincing that I shouted. The whisper and echoes of the trees changed to laughter and mourning, and the eyes of the forest stretched open, and its limbs reached out to grab me from Papa's tight grasp. I closed my eyes tightly and my head bounced against his chest and shoulder.

"Run!" he said again, encouraging Torma and Ol' Ma not to stop, no matter how painful, no matter how far the earth stretched its hands from the tree stumps to pull their legs and lappas back.

"I coming," my Ol' Ma said with the hardness of a rainy season storm, past Papa, with eyes too focused on the end to cry, and a story that meant too much to her to risk ending now.

FOUR

Before the dragon came—a thing, not a person—before Hawa Undu was born, humans ruled the forest. Gola people and Kissi people and Loma people and Gio people. Vai people and Kpelle people and Kru people and Mano people. Bassa people and Krahn people and Grebo people and Gbani people. And these groups, they all ruled in their own way, prayed in their own way, told stories in their own way, loved in their own way. The people had many chiefs and each group had one prince to lead them. But the dragon said the forest was too small, and the ways of the people were not correct, not what the dragons did on the other side of Mami Wata's shoulders. So. They said no more chiefs no more princes. No more praying no more speaking in those ways. There is one correct way to tell a story, the dragon said. The people fell in line, but those princes never stopped being. Death is not the end. And after that dragon had spent a long time ruling the forest, telling the people the correct ways, princes began to fight. None of them won, but soon a man who used to be a dragon's soldier rose up. One from the Krahn people. This man promised that the forest would be for everyone again. That there were many different ways to tell a story. Some believed him and were glad, but the faith did not last. Those promises broke into tiny pieces. Papa said it would not be long until this man was gone and order would be restored. Others, like our neighbors, like my schoolmates, like my uncles, believed the forest would die and it was time to find another home, so they left. This soldier man who entered the forest had become a dragon himself, but the most curious kind, one who did not understand the fire within. So when the dragon heard that yet another prince was entering the forest, this one with his own soldiers, this one of Gola blood whose family had come long ago from America, the dragon used the fire too much. The Krahn people from which the dragon came were ashamed. And those the dragon hated most, whose princes had opposed him, the Gio people and Mano people, were also ashamed, were afraid.

Outside of the woods that day as we hurried to Pastor's house, it was suddenly clear who was Krahn: those most afraid of rebels. And it was clear who was Gio and who was Mano: those most afraid of the dragon's soldiers, the ones wearing army uniforms in the distance. The Gio and Mano walked faster, gazed at the ground, eyes as though they had been crying, avoiding the gaze of those who could have been the army men sent to kill them.

Papa led us to Pastor's house immediately after departing the woods. The house—like all of the houses in Caldwell—sat on its own separate hill with a cement porch in the front, a wooden deck in the back, and a garden on both sides visible from the main road. People rushed past his house, some the dragon's people, some running, as we entered.

A man and a woman ran across the porch and into his house, with a pace as urgent as Papa and Ol' Ma's after the drums made us run through the woods.

"What were those?" I whispered to Torma.

"Guns."

"What are guns?"

"What the rebels fight with. How they beat the drums."

"For how long?"

"Until the war finish."

I imagined the rebels were walking around pounding the drums with their guns and sticks and sugarcane. I wondered who was at the front of the line as they marched to fight. Did he have to beat his gun the loudest?

Inside the house, Pastor's living room was filled with people who sat on his sofas and blue rugs. Against the wall there was a large bookcase with books and pictures of memories with his family and friends. A few children sat against the bookcase with sandwich bags of Kool-Aid that were tied at the opening. A small hole was cut in the corner of the bag where the children sucked the juice out.

Pastor's wife met Papa at the front door as she cradled and rocked her young daughter, who cried because of the sound of those drums outside. Pastor's wife was a tall woman with a pretty face who walked like her shoulders were trying to touch her chest.

"Gus," she said, touching Papa's arm after he put K and me on the floor. "Thank God you made it. Pastor is in the kitchen with the others." She placed her hand on each of our heads and hugged Ol' Ma and Torma before leaving.

Papa pointed to an empty corner in the room and Ol' Ma led us there through the crowd. Torma followed the pastor's wife and tapped her on the shoulder, as she bent down toward a woman who ranted that her husband was not at home when she and her son left.

"You know where I can find water? For the girls?" Torma asked.

"Go in the kitchen. We ran out of cups, so you can put it in a bag and tie it," she said, shaken.

I searched through the breaks in the crowd for Papa. First for his body. Then for his voice. In the kitchen Pastor and a few deacons sat down at the table in front of glasses of water that shook when the drum beating and the gun beating was too loud outside. Pastor looked young, like Moneysweet young, even though we all called him Pastor, and he always wore a shirt made of country cloth with colors that looked like a kaleidoscope. One of the deacons could not sit still in his chair, as if his okra stew was taking too long to arrive, and the rough hairs of his chest were wet, and you could see it all because his shirt was unbuttoned. His glasses had thick frames that rode up and down his nose with each word.

"You all good?" Pastor asked Papa. One deacon stood up and shook Papa's hand.

"Yeh," Papa said. "Moneysweet gone. Torma and Ma with us."

"Good."

"They were past the bridge when we left. The bullets reached the house."

"The people serious. War is here," the deacon said, folding his hands at the table.

Torma handed Papa a plastic bag of cold water on her way back to the living room. He took the bag and cut through the corner with his teeth to drink.

"What do you make of it?" Papa asked.

"Me, I going. Some boy passing told me people going to the ETMI to wait. The government set up camp there already," a man said.

"That's not far from here," Papa said of the school. Outside the windows, carloads of escapers filled the streets. Some were barefoot, like they had dropped everything they were doing and left. Others had suitcases or bags of belongings, the things they could not live without spilling out of the plastic. Ol' Mas balanced bundles of clothes and other effects on their heads, their children and grandchildren running behind them.

"No, it's not far," a deacon affirmed.

"How many people you got here?" Papa asked Pastor.

"I didn't count. They come and go. The house is open," Pastor said.

"We can go toward the river," a man shouted. "Another boy said they got ships leaving for Sierra Leone."

"You go toward the river you have to pass too much bush. Rebels them in the bush looking for people to recruit to fight," a man argued. "Your children not safe. They will kill you and take your children."

I saw Papa sit down. I did not understand what they were saying. It was the language the old ones spoke, foreign words and meanings, and I only wanted to see Mam.

"The people already set up refugee camps in Guinea and Ivory Coast is what I hear people saying on the road," a deacon said. "It will be safer there for those of you who got children."

"You go through all that trouble and what happens if they kill Doe next week?" a man argued. "This thing will not last. Hide small and the thing will be over soon."

"It's different-oh," Papa said. "This is not small thing. The rebels on the road near the bridge. They're young boys with guns too big for their own self to hold. They don't look all right."

"Yeh," some others agreed.

"That's big thing here. Not next week thing-oh. If you can leave the country, go."

"Ah!" a woman shrieked in the living room as a loud bang outside shook the picture frames in the display case she sat underneath. Seconds later, another blast sounded in the distance.

"Where is Mam?" I asked close to my Ol' Ma's chest.

"We going. We going to her."

With the third drum, glass shattered in the den and screams flooded the house.

"They shooting," a deacon said, rushing out of the kitchen. Papa followed him and came to us.

"Let's go," he said to Ol' Ma.

"Where?" she asked, lifting us from the ground.

"The ETMI. The school," he said.

"Yeh, go," Pastor said to Papa. "We will meet you all there."

Papa took us from the corner where we huddled with Ol' Ma and Torma. Everyone was rushing again and it confused me. Who were we running from? The dragon? The prince? We hurried out of Pastor's front door in a greater hurry than when we walked in. The road north out of Caldwell that would lead us out of Monrovia was a long and narrow cement road with tall weed bushes and sugarcane fields on either side.

"Papa, where we going?" I asked him.

"Away," he said, eyes glued to the road and the people who slowly flooded it.

K remained in Papa's arms and laid her head against his shoulder. She looked as confused as I felt, as more people crowded the road. Wi and I walked on either side of Ol' Ma and I squeezed her hand in my fingers like the bread dough Korkor once allowed us to play with when she became too tired to yell at us to stop running around the house. Men, women, and children peeked their heads out of the sugarcane fields before walking out onto the road to join us. There were some who were barefoot, and their walking became jogging when any noise or crack sounded in the distance. Many women traveled with mountains of belongings tied into bundles on their backs and heads, keeping their balance as the bundles wobbled high into the air. Some walked with nothing in their hands.

"Where we going?" I asked again.

"Yeh, where?" Wi echoed, moving closer to Ma as more people joined the road out of Monrovia.

"Away," Papa answered.

"For how long?" Wi asked.

"I will tell you all soon. Not very long," he said in one breath.

"And we will see Mam soon?" I asked.

"We will see Mam soon."

"We going to America?" I asked.

"No, no, not America," Papa stuttered. "But we will see her soon."

"Can we go back for my doll baby?" K whined into Papa's neck, tears now rusted on her cheeks.

"Maybe. We will see," Papa said.

Questions waited at the roof of my mouth. Just as I was about to begin asking, as the words attempted to seep through the thin spaces between my teeth and fall at Papa's feet, he stopped walking and waved his arm in the air.

"What is it?" Ol' Ma asked in a panic before she noticed that the expression on Papa's face was one of relief.

"James!" he yelled. "James? Brother James!"

Some of the people in front of us ducked for cover, others ran back into the field for fear that the yelling was a warning of dangers. Fifty feet ahead of us, a man turned around, and after noticing Papa, he hurried toward us through the crowd.

"Brother James!" Papa yelled as the man approached.

"Mr. Moore!" he replied as he reached Papa and hugged him. He was a man with narrow shoulders, taller and younger than Papa, and he lived by himself not too far from our house. We saw him at church and he always had candy to give us.

"You well, enneh-so?" Papa asked, patting his shoulder.

"Yeh," Brother James answered. He picked me up and I felt his body shake.

"The drums?" I asked him after I saw he was startled by the outlying drums. Brother James looked at me and at Papa. Their exchange was cut short when Brother James said:

"Yes. Drumbeats."

"Why they so loud?" Wi asked Papa.

"I don't know," Papa said.

"We must hurry-oh. I want make it to de ETMI before dark. They now set up camp there with food," Brother James said. I remembered driving by the big school they spoke of many times.

"Yeh. That's where we going," Papa nodded and we continued to walk, the crowd of people now nearly shoulder to shoulder as we headed out of Monrovia.

"I'm hungry," K began.

Papa handed her to Ma and he stopped in the middle of the road. He knelt down and opened the small backpack that he had taken from the house and pulled out a pack of crackers. The crowd shuffled around us. He opened the pack and gave a couple of crackers to K, then to Wi and me.

As I raised the cracker to my mouth, almost tasting the salt on my tongue, another drum, louder than all the rest, was struck so hard that I dropped my cracker on the road.

"Come," Papa said, placing the bag back on his shoulder. Papa ran, pulling my hand as I was dragged behind him. Everyone on the road was running, screaming. After a hundred yards he stopped, looking in the distance in the direction of the drum.

"You can walk now. Walk now, but quickly," he coaxed as K began to cry again.

"The rebels now block off the east and south borders," Brother James said.

"How you know?" Papa asked him.

"I started walking toward there to take bus out of Liberia to Ghana. I got family there," he said, still trembling, I could tell, though I was no longer touching him. "They will question you if they know your job. I saw them stopping people who look like they work for the government. Even on the road."

Papa worked for the government, for the water and sewer company, but he was not Krahn like Hawa Undu and his people. Brother James said people like the rebels would think Papa supported Hawa Undu because of his government job.

"Good thing Ol' Ma with you. Even if they don't bother you for job, they still see Congo man."

"Yes. And I got my university ID for the class I teach. I will say I'm a teacher," Papa said. Brother James nodded.

"What is this ETMI business?" Papa asked, changing the subject, eyeing the travelers around us.

"Camp. I will not stay there long. I want get news from there."

"Then where you will go?" Papa asked.

"I don't know yet," Brother James answered.

The roads looked different when traveled on foot. I realized I did not usually pay attention to what was happening outside of my car seat, where I would have pinching contests with my sisters to see who squeezed hardest, leaving throbbing red circles across our forearms. On foot the road was bumpy, full of rocks and now clothes that had fallen from the duffles of others who had left. Some shirts of different colors, some American shirts with the faces of American people smiling with their happy teeth and powdered skin. The crowd grew around us and my steps were closer and closer together. I squeezed Papa's hand. Then I pulled it until he looked down. When I finally had his attention, I said nothing. I just stared at him, nearly stumbling along as we walked.

"What?" Papa asked after too long had passed without any words. "We will be there soon," he said.

"And we will see Mam," I said.

"Yes," he said, before quickly looking away.

So my eyes returned to the road and those in front of us. There were Ol' Mas and Ol' Pas with canes, wobbling slowly to balance bags over their shoulders and atop their heads. They were with their children, and their grandchildren, who all carried heavier bags, looking nervously out into the fields and crowd, some with stains of tears covering their faces.

There were sugarcane fields on either side of us, the stalks like skinny bamboo at the roots and the brightest green at the crowns. It was rainy season and it had poured heavily only a few short days before, so I jumped over tiny puddles across the wide dirt road. I counted the puddles as we passed them. Sometimes I jumped over them and sometimes Papa lifted my arm so that my entire body flew over the dead water.

I had counted enough puddles when from behind I was pushed to the ground. A small boy and his mother rushed past me. Papa grabbed my arm and lifted me up, while some women who traveled behind us screamed. I turned around and four men, the prince's men, rebels, moved through the crowd with long pipes the color of stones. Were those guns? They held them close to their bodies with straps that hung like purses, and none of them had drums. They were wearing plain clothes, dirty clothes, not uniforms, so they were not Hawa Undu's men; they did not fight for the Armed Forces of Liberia (AFL). They fought for the prince. They were not taller than my father. The boys looked younger than Moneysweet, and fire and sparks spurted out of the mouths of their guns. Another ran out of the sugarcane field pointing his gun toward the crowd. We were near the front of the crowd and the rebels approached from the back.

"Hands up!" he yelled.

Those who were running stopped.

"Lift your hands," Papa said and I raised my hands in the air, copying the others around me. I did not understand why the boys were pointing their guns at us or what we had done wrong. Or where the drums were that they used to make the sounds. Papa was a good man. Many people told him this. And I thought I was a good girl, and always apologized when I pinched too hard and one of my sisters cried.

"Don't cry," Papa whispered to me.

"Walk!" one of the boys yelled.

So the crowd continued, all of us, with our hands raised in the air and their guns to our backs.

"You all government people here? Where the government people?" one of them asked, his voice a boulder, his words so close together it was difficult to understand. He spoke like those who lived outside of Monrovia. At the pastor's house the women said that is where the prince found some of his boys to fight for him.

"Who government?" another one asked, poking the gun into the backs of members of the crowd, some of them begging and covering their heads. All of them had big eyes, sharp teeth and moved like they were playing football, chasing a moving target, but nothing was on the ground.

The rebels moved closer to us from the back of the crowd. Papa worked for the government. I looked at him, watched his face for what would happen next.

"Look ahead," Papa said, low so only we could hear him. "Just keep your hands up, keep walking and looking ahead."

The drums were loud in the distance and each step felt like an entire day had passed us. The many feelings of a whole day wrapped into those waiting moments, as the rebels got closer. What would Papa say when they reached him? Would they recognize him?

"You all come!" one of the rebels yelled from behind. "Government soldiers them not far." We heard the others stop, their feet shuffling as they changed directions, only a few feet away from Papa. He sighed, and I heard Ol' Ma release a short murmur, wrapped in a prayer. The rebels turned around and as quickly as they'd come, they disappeared into the sugarcane field toward the sound of the drums.

When we could no longer hear them, almost at once everyone started to run. Papa held my hand, dragging me. I lost my breath in the rainy season puddles, sobbed into the backs of those drums until I was blinded by the tears, and fear, so crippling that I was not sure if this was a bad dream that Torma or Korkor would eventually wake me up from. Every few steps I could feel the sharp end of a stone tear through my slippers, and I thought of Mam. If she knew what would happen here. If she knew that we were running. And as if I had been pinched, too hard to keep from crying, I realized that I would not be home that Sunday when Mam called. The phone would ring and still ring and we would not answer to tell her about the drums. Or that we had been running but we had been good. That the rebels almost asked Papa where he worked but they ran away first, and I saw Papa's eyes go back to the time Mam got on that plane, dark, as if he was struggling to see something too far ahead.

When Papa said we were close to the ETMI where we would rest, and far enough from the rebels, he let us slow down. We walked until we could see the sun at the end of the road. We traveled toward it, taking turns sitting on Papa and Ol' Ma's hips.

"I want to go home," K whined.

"Soon, soon," Papa said. In the evening as we approached the ETMI, the crowd began to move slower in front of us.

"We here," Brother James said. A sign on the gate read: Elizabeth Tubman Memorial Institute. When the people walking in front of us scattered and our view of the institute was clear, Papa squeezed my hand in his.

"Ay God," Ma said with her hand over her heart.

Before us, seated on the courtyard of the ETMI and spilling out of the building behind it, to the side of it on the tennis court and soccer field, and behind it, was what looked like everybody in the country. Everybody in Liberia, all the people in one place, on that field, away from the forest.

"Eight thousand and counting," Brother James said.

"Oh God," Ma said again.

Men and older boys stood together on the edge of the courtyard in conversations as deep and with faces as long as Papa had when the deacons came to visit Caldwell. People lay on small bags of folded clothes and attempted sleeping.

"Stay close. Don't let go of each other's hands," Papa said as he led us through the crowd toward the building. Inside, mostly women and children occupied the complex. The dragon's men patrolled the building with rifles, and older women served small cups of dry white rice to a line that wrapped around the interior walls of the complex and continued out of and around the building.

"'Scuse me," Papa said, touching a soldier as we entered the building. The soldier looked at Papa like he had done a bad thing. Papa pulled his hand away.

"What?" the soldier shouted, the whites of his eyes red and yellowed, his mustache and beard coiled into small balls of hair that wanted nothing to do with each other.

"Do you know when we will be able to return?" Papa asked, nicer than I had ever heard him talk.

The soldier's lip curled and he did not answer Papa.

"Can you give me estimate of how long they will take to capture the rebels?" he asked.

"You want go home, go home," the soldier yelled and hissed his teeth at Papa. He spit on the ground before walking away, his gun pointed out into the air by his side. Brother James touched Papa's shoulder.

"Come, man. They don't know what's going on either, and you don't want to raise suspicion. Let's just go rest. We will find out what's happening in the morning."

I had never heard anyone talk to Papa that way, or walk away from him before he finished speaking. He did not move for long after that. He stood looking in the direction of the soldier.

"Let's go," Papa said finally, and led us to a corner inside the complex. There were stains on his shirt from the dust on the road and his clothes smelled sour with sweat.

"What are you doing?" another soldier yelled as Papa and Brother James cleared the space in the corner for us to sit.

"Men not allowed here to rest. You sleep outside," he said as he moved toward us.

"Okay," Brother James said quickly, like he was afraid of the soldier.

"On the tennis court!" the soldier yelled. He stood and waited for Papa and Brother James to follow him.

"Stay with them, yeh? We will be right outside," Papa told Ol' Ma before kissing her on the cheek. "Right by the door."

Ma nodded, and she looked as if she would cry.

"Where you going?" I asked, grabbing Papa's arm.

"I will be right outside," Papa said over the noisiness of the crowd.

"I want to come with you," I pleaded.

"Let's go!" the soldier screamed. Other men with rifles looked his way.

"Come on," Brother James said to Papa.

"I want to come!" I cried.

Torma pulled me away from Papa as he disappeared with Brother James through the crowd and out of the complex to the tennis court.

Ma and Torma pulled us in.

"Nah-mah," Torma said. Never mind. "Nah-mah, yeh?"

Ol' Ma hummed and her voice formed a shield around us. In the corners, trash hung around each trash bin—there were too many people in the school and loose paper, lost clothing. The floors were covered with lappas, where other women like my Ol' Ma sat with small children, silent as they cried, voices gone after those lies of going back home soon soon.

"Where is Mam?" I asked and missed her smell. "Where is Mam?" I asked again but no one answered. Perhaps I was dreaming and when I woke up I would continue watching my American film as Moneysweet cut the rosebush outside and Korkor washed the lunch greens at the sink and Torma braided Wi's hair as I danced. And Papa would read to me in the evening before calling Mam in New York and I would tell her how well I was doing. Perhaps this was only a long journey to market and the sounds outside were only festival drums and something bad happened at the festival and that was why everybody had to come to this place, but tomorrow we would be dancing together because maybe this was a surprise for us since they liked giving us surprises when we least expected it.

Or maybe since everyone kept saying Hawa Undu's name, at the pastor's house and on the road, then at that moment the prince and his men surrounded the forest and Hawa Undu was shaking now, hiding underneath a fallen branch so that the rebels would not see his scales.

At dawn a woman screamed. It was a shriek, a painful sound that made some duck for cover and others awake from their sleep. She cried while she screamed, a continuous sound that I heard in my dreams. She said her daughter was stolen in the night and was convinced that it was a soldier at the ETMI, certain that some of them were rebels in disguise. She was so ruined that she searched the corners and splayed lappas on the floors while calling her daughter's name. Ol' Ma stood up as soon as she understood what the woman implied happened to her daughter. She raised us to our feet, folding her lappa and placing it back in a bag that hung at her waist. I had never seen her look so desperate, so furious.

"Come, come," she said. "Come now."

She picked up K and grabbed my hand.

"Hold Wi's hand tight," she said to Torma, who, though confused and with eyes that had only just adjusted to morning, obeyed.

We hurried through the crowd to the tennis court outside. Soldiers stood in clusters on the edges of the court. We were at the doorway for less time than it took to walk outside before Papa and Brother James came running to us. Their clothes were wet and the air still held a mist from the overnight storm.

"What happened?" Papa asked.

"They stealing children. One woman said they stole her daughter," Ol' Ma said. I could tell that she intended to whisper or conceal the end of her sentence, to hide the words from us, but her fear could not be hidden. I had heard and felt it too—the beating of her heart. That desperate pace.

"Come," Papa said, and took K from Ol' Ma.

"But we will miss the food here," Torma said, under her breath.

"We should go," Papa said. "It is not safe here."

I did not want to be at the ETMI since hearing that story. But Torma was right. I was hungry and I was tired and I missed Mam more than I knew I could. And it was only morning but the drums had already begun to tell that day's story.

FIVE

Since most people who had left their houses in Monrovia neighborhoods that week stayed at the ETMI, at dawn we walked alone. We did not have the dry rice they fed us at the school or the crackers Papa grabbed from our pantry before leaving, so he walked into sugarcane fields and retrieved sticks of sugarcane for us to eat. We chewed and sucked the juice for energy, then spit out the hard sticks on the dirt roads.

Later in the day when we heard the sound of car wheels, or if someone yelled "rebel," we ran into the cane fields and hid. The canes from the field were sharp and as it became later in the day, our legs were covered with scratches. The stalks were not so tall that we could stand and avoid being seen, so we knelt on the ground together; I made sure that I was touching Papa every time, either his fingers or his shirt as he breathed loudly between stalks.

Other times I sat on his shoulder as we walked. The breeze was calmer from where I sat, but it was there that I noticed the people lying on the road.

"Why is everyone lying down?" I asked Papa.

"They are asleep," he said. "You cannot sleep right now, because we have to go see Mam."

First there were only a few, sprinkled here and there, surrounded by dark red puddles. Then on some roads there were many. I saw an old man and woman, I saw some boys, some men, then I saw a family resting—a mother and father and four children—surrounded by a deep red color, their clothes scattered around them.

When Papa saw that the sun was setting, he looked for places for us to sleep, afraid to travel with three young girls and Torma in the middle of the night.

"We have to find somewhere before it gets dark-oh," Brother James said.

"I know. I looking," Papa said.

"What you looking for?" I asked Papa as I sat on his shoulders and surveyed the countryside.

He thought hard.

"A house," he said.

"An-nen we will go see Mam?" K asked. "We will go to our house?"

"Our house?" Wi asked excitedly.

He waited again.

"No. Another house," he said. "But then we will go back."

"How long?" I asked.

"Be strong for Papa. Be strong, yeh? Tell me . . . tell me the story of Jonah."

"Once upon a time there was a man," Wi said, smiling.

"—from Ninevah!" I interrupted her.

"He ran from God and the big big whale swallowed him."

"A real whale?" K asked, always, although she had heard the story countless times.

"A house!" Brother James said.

"Where?" Papa asked.

"There," he said, pointing to a house that sat like an ant separated from its colony, tired of wandering, waiting alone to die.

By the time we reached the house, it was almost night and I could barely make out the faces of my family. The small house sat about fifty yards from the road. The front door was opened, the windows were shattered, and broken pieces of glass covered the porch where a rocking chair moved slowly in the evening breeze.

"Wait here with them," Papa said to Ol' Ma as he and Brother James headed into the house.

"I want go," I said.

"Stay here with Ma," he said sternly. Papa and Brother James lumbered through the unkempt grass. They disappeared behind the distressed wood.

"What they looking for?" Wi asked, pulling Torma's hand.

"Rebels," Torma said.

"What rebels?" Wi asked.

Papa ran out of the house and back to the road.

"Come," he said, picking up K. We followed him through the yard. He kicked the broken glass out of our way and we plodded across the porch and into the house.

"Hold my hand," he said. Ma held his hand and mine, I held Torma's, and Torma held Wi's. Linked, we moved through the dark house to a back corner where moonlight bled through.

"It stinks," I said, wrinkling my nose to what smelled like molded cheese.

"Torma, go try find running water," Ma whispered.

"Where? You want me find well?" Torma asked.

"No, just find kitchen."

"Come," Papa told her and she hesitantly walked with him out of the room. "Stay here with Brother James," he told us. We found the corner of the room beneath the moonlight, where we sat near Brother James and hugged Ma in the dark. We heard a flow of water in the other room.

"Sounds like they found water," Brother James said under his breath and stood up, but remembering that we were alone in the room, he paced around where we sat until Papa returned.

"Water is there. Torma will wash the clothes and when she finishes James and I will wash."

"Oh praise God," Ma said.

We followed her in the dark toward the sound of the running water.

During the day we walked, during the night Papa and Brother James found old, abandoned houses for us to sleep in. They always came back to the road to get us, and we entered the dark houses and slept close to Ol' Ma, as the sounds of panic and unrest shook the roads nearby. One day, Papa took longer than usual to return to the road.

"Maybe I should go in," Torma said as we waited together for Papa and Brother James to return.

"No," Ma answered her. "You hear that?"

We became quiet and could then hear a voice that was neither Papa nor Brother James.

"I should go," Torma said louder.

"Pray the devil back to hell," Ma whispered, pulling us all toward her. "No, wait here with them," she told Torma.

Ma went toward the house. She searched the yard and picked up a large stick from the trash on the front lawn.

"Shh," Torma said as our whimpers formed, although I felt her arms shudder as she hugged us.

Ma prayed out loud as she tiptoed toward the door with the stick in her hand.

"Oh God come be with us-oh," she said. "God come help us-oh, God come give me strength-oh."

As Ma staggered to the porch, Papa finally appeared. Taken aback, he laughed when he saw her with the stick. She angrily threw it back into the grass and squeezed her lappa.

"What you take so long for?" she yelled at him.

We ran to them and Papa put his arm around Ma.

"Sorry," he said, "but look."

From the darkness, a family of four emerged onto the porch.

"They were hiding here and thought we were rebels," Papa said.

"Ay-yah," Ma said, shaking the woman's hand. She touched her palm to the woman's face, as if she had known her for a very long time.

"Hello, Ol' Ma," the woman said.

"Come, let's go inside," Papa said.

The woman looked Torma's age and wore a dress with short sleeves that revealed her arms, which looked like two long sticks. They had two sons, boys the same height who looked older than my sisters and me and looked as if they had been punished for a crime only the worst people would commit.

"What happened to your eye?" I asked one of the boys when I noticed that one of his eyes was swollen shut.

"Apollo," his mother said.

"Apollo?" I asked.

"Something you get from being in the sun for long," Papa said tapping my shoulder to be quiet. "The people call it apollo."

"How long you all been here?" Ol' Ma asked them.

"Two days. I want his eye to get well before we leave again," the man said.

"Where you people from?" the father asked.

"Caldwell," Papa answered. "And you?"

"Bong County," he said.

This house did not have a smell. It did not feel abandoned, either; it felt as though the family was welcoming us in as guests to a place that had been theirs for a long time.

"Where you all going?" the man asked Papa.

"We trying reach the north border. I hear the rebels them not there much yet. We want to go to Sierra Leone," he answered. "And you?"

"That's where we were headed but we turned around. We will try to make it to Guinea instead," the father said. "I heard on the road they're not letting men cross into Sierra Leone. The Sierra Leone government doesn't want to risk letting rebels or spies in and spreading the war."

It was dark but I could almost see Papa's disappointment.

"Not letting people in?" Brother James asked.

"No," the man said, certainly. "It's risky for them, so only women and children for now."

"We will turn around? To go where?" Torma asked.

"Nah-mah," Ol' Ma said. "Gus, we can go to Lai then."

Papa turned to her.

"Lai?" he asked.

Ol' Ma nodded and pulled me close, hugging my shoulder. Lai was a village hidden by the forests. It was Ol' Ma's village—where she lived before meeting Ol' Pa, before moving into the city so they could find work and educate Mam and her sisters. Mam says they took us all to Lai as babies, to show Ol' Ma's family, but we had not visited since, though Mam and her sisters, my aunts, talked about it often.

In order to get to Lai, Mam once said, we would have to travel on a canoe. She told me that I would enjoy this canoe, because the canoe traveled along a lake so clear that we would see our reflections, and every hair on our head could be counted on the face of the water.

"That's where the Ol' Pa and the others in Logan Town probably hiding. And the rebels won't find it," Ol' Ma added. "We will have to find somebody to take us in the canoe."

"Yes, we can go to Lai then," Papa nodded, as if the idea were his, and I could tell he was still thinking. "We will wait for a few weeks for the boys to get out of Monrovia."

"And you will go back? Liberia won't be same for long time-oh!" the man said.

"We will see," Papa said. "But Lai is good choice. Rebels will not find it easily."

Papa continued his conversation with the man and Brother James, and we moved to the back of the room and sat down on a floor near the window.

"I have apple," the woman said, rushing to a corner where a dim glare from an old lantern provided us light.

"We found some here. You all want?" she asked.

We looked at Ol' Ma and waited for her. When she nodded her head, we grabbed the apples and devoured them. They were so sweet. So delicious. The woman smiled at Torma.

"How old are they?" she asked.

"This one just turned four, and these two are five and six," Ol' Ma answered. "Their mother is in America."

"Oh," the woman said, examining our clothes, as if she gathered that we were from the city. She pulled the son with the swollen eye close to her and stroked his head. The boy's eye watered and he sniffed. They were all dry with hunger and exhaustion, beaten by the war outside. I wondered if we looked the same way.

"How old?" Ol' Ma asked her.

"Nine and seven," the woman answered, then without warning began to cry.

"Ay-yah. Nah-mah," Ol' Ma said softly. "This thing, like all bad things. It will end soon."

Her sons just stared at her helplessly, as if they were used to her crying and knew that nothing could be done but to wait.

"I know, I pray for it," the woman said. "I had another. But . . ."

Ol' Ma pressed her hand against her heart. She waited for the woman to continue.

The mother said that her other son was thirteen years old and she was at home with her sons three weeks before when the rebels invaded their county. Her husband was not at home when she saw others leaving, when she saw them packing their belongings and fleeing on the roads. Some people were headed to Guinea, and others decided they would walk toward Monrovia since the rebels had not reached there yet, and they hoped the dragon's men could possibly fight and defeat the uprising. She was not sure which way to go and was afraid her husband would not know where to find her, so she stayed in the house. When she heard the caravan of rebels close by, she told her sons to hide around the house, in the kitchen and in the bathroom, and she tried to hide under the bed, but two rebels found her. She became silent then and her tears were more abundant.

"Nah-mah," Ol' Ma said.

"What happened when the rebels came?" I asked. "What happened?"

"They were unkind," Ol' Ma said. "They hurt her."

"It was too long. I don't know how long and my own son, the thirteen-year-old, he came in the room and told them he would go with them if they left me alone. So they took him and I cried for him to stay but he went with them. The next day my husband came back and we left but I don't know what happened to my son. My husband said the rebels will force him to fight. But he is no fighter. He is a gentle boy. Brave but gentle. Now I don't know what happened to him."

"Ay God," Ol' Ma said and murmured a prayer for the woman. I wondered whether, if Mam was there, if she would hide like the woman did. I was happy she was not there, because I did not want the rebels to hurt her if they found her. But if they tried to, I would be like the woman's son and run to where she was and hug her, and tell them not to hurt Mam.

"I hear it will take long for them to move the rebels," I could hear the man say to Papa. "The people say leave the country until Taylor and the rebels move Doe from the mansion."

"For true?" Brother James said.

"Yeh."

"They want Doe to surrender. Taylor came with plenty boys," the man said. Papa opened his mouth but nothing came out. He wanted to argue as he always did when the dragon's name came up, I could tell. But he could not.

Papa listened to us talk to God that night and breathed into the wincing shadows on the wall. Afterward, he, Brother James, and the man walked to the front door. I fell asleep to their whispers near the entrance and woke up to the same.

SIX

My eyes were heavy and I could not look at the sun because it was no longer yellow like in our picture books with dancing girls and boys who held hands around a world too small for people it looked orange from where I stood and it burned when I looked up and so I did not orange in a white sky made my eyes heavy and because I could not look at the sun since I could not envision my face in the clouds with purple and orange barrettes bouncing up and down on a couch I should not have been bouncing up and down was a restless head or Popsicles or sunflowers or other things the clouds never made I stopped but they commanded that I keep walking and I did since stopping would mean spending more than three seconds near the sleeping bodies with frozen faces the boy with the bright blue shirt the ones who striped the streets and seeded the farm roads with no destination in sight but tears that fell under an open sun we walked and did not know where we were going tired the heat and betrayed by nightly prayers unanswered it seemed and "Where we going?" I asked and nowhere was their answer though it did not make sense that we were making such a fuss on a journey that was not somewhere and "Where is Mam?" I asked and we are going to see her and I stopped counting the days forgot what Mam's voice sounded like they did not know which soldiers were good and which were rebels could not hand us punishments for our whining for fear it would be our last did not know where we were going so I cut my eyes and slowed down and "Come now, keep up" is from Ol' Ma who acted like she did not see the bodies or did not smell what smelled like blood or did not care that I had stopped walking because it hurt to look up at the orange sun and clouds that drew nothing but rain my left shoe fell off and I wanted Ol' Ma to notice but she did not so I kicked off my right shoe and it hit her heel in front of me and she turned around but instead of picking up my shoe and demanding the entire caravan to "STOP AT ONCE" walking to this nowhere she pulled my hand to keep up with her and "Come now, keep up" sounded like those guns beating against something too hard as we strolled between those men and women like crooked lines and shapes sleeping they told us dreaming of heaven now they told us under the open sun my feet were bare and I did not tell Papa because I was afraid he would not know what to say I did not tell Wi or K because I was afraid they would tell Papa so I walked—with Papa and the girls and Ma and Torma and two pastors and a neighbor and some members of our church under an orange sun and clouds to nowhere we were walking I was barefoot down this dusty road of bodies and the boy with the bright blue shirt and broken stories and pretending they all and none of them were there Pastor Brown pointed to something approaching us in the distance it was a tank they said it was a tank and in one second my frail body was in two places one was on the road one was jumping over the bodies gone to heaven now two and I was we were off the road and my bare feet were being dragged through a muddy field and (where were my shoes) as K cried and I wondered what I did to the sun for it to hate me as it did and the monstrous stalks were slapped with bullets and talking leaves said run and do not look back and blood poured out of the bottom of my feet as thorns pushed their way in and running and running and Papa was moving so fast and pulling my hand that the muddy waters were now my pool my baptism into one second past girlhood past innocence past things the clouds never made and my feet lost the ground beneath me so my knees now ran along with Papa and water now ran along my face and the lace at the bottom of my dress got left somewhere behind me with my shoes and the tank and my girlhood and the shooting that did not stop but came toward me under the open orange suns and clouds that said nothing more than rain.

SEVEN

They found little girls' shoes in an abandoned house, mismatching slippers and sneakers and church shoes that Papa insisted we wear even though I cried that it was painful to walk with them on. We were only three days away from a town called Junde, where we would catch a canoe that would take us to the village Lai.

"It's not safe to walk with no shoes on. The glass in the road will cut you," Papa had said.

The outer layers of my feet were swollen and shredded from the sugarcane field thorns. Each step made my stomach turn and hurt, and that feeling traveled to my head. The sting was so serious that it felt like all of the water in my body left me from my eyes, and the river left a trail on the road out of Monrovia.

Since Papa was already holding K, who slept through the disorder in a small space underneath his chin, Brother James picked me up on his hip to ease my soreness.

The farther north we walked with our countrymen out of Monrovia, the more of us crowded the exploded pavement—shoeless and shirtless—faces smeared with all of the changes only three weeks had caused.

We walked underneath the sun. Brother James, whose once-shiny dress shoes had now dulled and lost their soles, limped as he held me; his steps were so inconsistent that on several occasions I nearly slid down his waist. The sun rays juked my eyes until I hid my face in Brother James's neck. A bitter smell seeped from his skin as he walked; he panted as if my body grew heavier in his arms.

When I awoke, the sun was almost gone and our company had stopped walking. Brother James put me down and held my hand as I rubbed my eyes beside him. The road was nearly empty, except for a few other escapers before us, and down the road Papa walked away from us, to a confrontation between a lone rebel and a man he recognized. Ma took my hand away from Brother James and pulled me and my sisters close to her, unsure whether she should hide in the sugarcane fields or continue behind Papa.

"James," she said.

"Wait here," Brother James told her and followed Papa. "The boy look high." The rebel, a boy around fourteen years old, no older than Torma, pointed a rifle at a man's head. He laughed as he did, a sound like razors cutting bones. The man stood on the sidelines, facing the road, his face covered with tears, his shirt stained with blood.

The boy wore camouflage trousers and black boots that were too large for his feet; he had a smug smile and eyes so red they looked like they were bleeding.

"I don't have money!" the man cried.

"Wait . . . wait," Papa said, approaching them. His hands were raised in the air. "Don't shoot!" he shouted. "Please don't shoot," Papa said again. From behind he looked different, smaller and as thin as the gun now pointed in his direction. "Here. Here, right here." Papa raised a crumbled wad of money from his pocket.

"Don't shoot," he said. The boy stared at the old five-dollar bill in the air. Papa threw the money on the ground in front of the rebel. The boy scuttled to pick up the pale green wad. He turned around and ran through an adjacent field. When he was out of sight, Papa ran to the man and hugged him.

"Amos!" he said. Amos collapsed in Papa's arms.

"Thank you. Thank you," he said, wiping his face. "He made me stand there all day."

"God bless you. Come," Papa said, picking up Amos.

"We got to hurry before he come back," Papa said, pulling us together. "He will come back." He motioned to us to keep walking and led us for another mile to a small shack in the back of a home that had been burned down. A family's memories were scattered in the mud. Inside, Papa and Brother James pushed a few yard tools to the back of the room, clearing space on the floor for us to sit. The cement was covered with ashes from the fire, along with coal, likely used to light a smoke pot that was nowhere to be found.

"It looks like they took everything here," Brother James said. He took an old towel from his bag and used it to push an empty frame and broken glass out of the shack. Amos still looked afraid and Brother James took a nearly empty bottle out of his bag of belongings to offer him. Amos drank the last of the bottle. I heard my Ol' Ma gulp, squeezing my shoulder. I knew she had hoped to share some with us that night.

Outside the shack it began to rain again, and I imagined in the recent past a family that lived in the incinerated home, only a dozen yards from where we sat. I saw their living room and den, their hallways and kitchen, and a bedroom where children played. I wondered where they were in that moment, if they were also resting on the cool and damp cement of a stranger's back house. Had they made it to Ghana? To Guinea? To Sierra Leone? Had they abandoned us here like the birds did? Like the planes did? Were they in America with Mam? I leaned into Ol' Ma and daydreamed to ease my hunger, the dryness that painted my throat, making it as hard to swallow as it now was to cry.

"I owe you, Gus," Amos said, finally catching his breath. Beneath his words, there were traces of his handsome, boyish face. "I will pay you back somehow."

"Nonsense," Papa said, sitting between Amos and Brother James across from us.

"I owe you, I owe you," Amos repeated.

Papa put his hand around Amos's shoulder. I wanted to go to him and hug him, but Ol' Ma held on to me, not letting me break free from her.

"You will be safe now," Papa said. "We will reach Junde day after tomorrow and we are taking a canoe to Lai to hide in Ma's village. At least until they stop fighting."

"How long have you been walking?" Amos asked.

"Three weeks. Almost."

"Aye! The girls them too," he shouted.

"Yeh, them too," Papa said.

Amos looked at the sores on our mouths, numb to me now, that had appeared within our first week from the sugarcane we ate for breakfast, lunch, and dinner.

"Sugarcane," Ma said, noticing his focus.

Amos shook his head.

"And you have not heard from Mam?" he asked.

"How?"

"I am not staying here," Amos said. "I am trying to get out."

"Borders closed," Brother James said.

"They are letting some people pass. Some. They didn't let me pass to Sierra Leone but I am going back toward Ghana to see if I can get across."

"Dangerous business," Papa said. "What news have you heard?"

"Doe is refusing to step down. Taylor and Prince Johnson got the rebels killing Krahn people and government people to force him to step down," he said.

There was salt in the following silence.

"Come with us to Lai, Amos," Papa said.

"You safer traveling with family, Amos. Government soldiers will mistake you for rebel, and rebels will try force you to join them or they will kill you," Brother James said.

Papa and Brother James and Amos, they talked all night about Liberia and her problems and all the things that could change her back to her old self. They talked about 1980 and 1983 and 1989. These men and their voices. And the memory of that rebel's voice—that stupid, insane boy, who, if he lived, would become a more stupid, more insane man. Men were talking plenty during this war. Men were deciding where to go and when to go and when to stop. They were deciding where to hide and what to eat and when to eat. They were deciding who would be killed and who would live. They were deciding which direction the planes would fly and when they would be removed from the sky. And they were dividing plates of not-enough food and leading the way. And those male dogs howling in the distance, bellies full of rotting male carcasses, as some rebel men decided who would cut their throats and roast them for that night's meal. And those men at the edge of the forest, those princes and rebels who wished to kill Hawa Undu. Why all this palaver over a hiding dragon? Why hadn't they just asked a woman, one like Mam, one of those women who could do anything, and go anywhere, to just go inside the forest and talk to Hawa Undu in a nice voice? To make him a feast and pepper his palm butter with those spices Mam used and feed him pork feet and dry fish like a king? And she would not fight him. She would just hold Hawa Undu's hand and lead him outside.

EIGHT

There was nowhere on our cream-colored walls in Caldwell too high for Papa to reach, no piece of furniture that he could not move with the slightest push. I would press my hand against his and it barely fit in his palm. Amazed, I looked past the dark veins of his stretched fingers and laughed with him as we guessed how many of my tiny hands could fit into his. Four was the decision. Once at our house in Caldwell, he told Wi, K, and me to stand together and hold each other as tightly as we could. Not knowing what to expect from the request, I hugged both of my sisters from either side. I grabbed their waists as they too grabbed mine. We huddled together and giggled over each other's shoulders, looking around nervously for him. From the hallway—he took measured strides in our direction with hunched shoulders and muscular limbs that dangled from each side.

"Rooooar," he said, making his way toward us.

We squealed and held on to each other as the giant approached.

"Rooooooooar," he said again, this time picking up his angled feet and running to where we stood.

He picked us up all at once. He twirled us around until our stomachs hurt from laughter. I held on to the girls as our heads bobbled high in the air. I saw the face of Moneysweet through the window, smiling. Korkor warned that he should not make us so dizzy that we would be sick for dinner. He continued, nonetheless, and we did not stop laughing until the fufu dropped into the stew of our stomachs at dinner that night.

Before Mam left for America, I saw him play the game with her one night. He captured her while she was in the kitchen cutting greens and threw her over his shoulder. Mam held her dress down as he balanced her over his shoulder. She screamed just as loudly as we did as he spun her around in midair and her hair draped toward the floor.

"P-put me down!" she chuckled, thrown over his shoulder.

Papa ran with her throughout the house, through the rooms and parlors, ran until he reached the den couch where he stopped and gently laid her down. She caught her breath from the hoots and giggles and pushed her hair back from over her face. The muscles in her neck tightened as she was getting ready to scold him, but Papa kissed her before she could speak, his shoulders dropped.

An aunty told a story once and let me listen. That Papa was not always as tall as he was during the years before the war. Was not always a big big man. Papa's Ma could not afford to keep him in her care. When he was a young child, his Ma took him to Virginia, Liberia, to live with his father and his father's wife. At seven years old he was a shy boy, and he stuttered, and his only friends were his half brother and half sister. In Virginia, Papa's family was part of the Congo middle class who owned stores and rubber farms, living better than those up-country, but still not as well as the Congo people in Monrovia.

"Gus," his stepmother called toward the small room where he slept. They said that Papa was led to the living room, where his father held two dogs. One was a white poodle that his sister ran to. The other was a black Labrador.

"Go." His father commanded the Labrador to go to Papa, who stood bravely still, although they say he was at first afraid. The dog went to Papa, first sniffing his feet and the ground around him, then working his nose up Papa's leg to the mangled shorts that hung from his slim waist. Certain that the only way to get over shaking in the dog's presence would be to hug him as his sister was doing, Papa extended his stiff hand into the air, ready for what was to come.

"What will you name them?" his stepmother had asked.

"Sugarlum," Papa's father said of the poodle.

"Sugarlum! Sugarlum!" Papa's sister blubbered happily and jumped around with the dog until it began to bark up at her and its tongue hung from the side of its mouth.

"And the other one?" his stepmother had asked, then looking at Papa and the black dog that now sat loyally by his side.

"Nobody," his father said without delay.

"What?"

"Nobody. The dog named Nobody," he chuckled to himself.

"Nobody?" his stepmother joined him laughing.

"Okay then, Nobody, take your dog and go get sugar for me from the neighbor," his stepmother joked playfully. The dog followed him. He smelled the road in front of Papa as he walked, with the front half of his body leading the way. The houses of Virginia were brick buildings that sat on several acres each, lining a paved road with residents carefully driven around by newly trained drivers, people from upcountry who recently moved into the cities for work.

When he reached the yard of the neighbor's house, he stopped and looked down at the black dog.

"Stay here," he said quietly. He turned from the dog but shortly after heard Nobody's heavy pants behind him. Papa stopped walking and held out his hand.

"Stay here," he said again, this time slightly louder than before. Nobody sat down in the grass. Again, Papa turned from the dog and headed toward the front door of the house. Also, again, Nobody followed him. Finally, Papa threw the stick in his hand. Nobody's head twisted toward the stick as it flew in the air and landed on the road behind him. He watched Papa approach the door and, instead of retrieving the stick, darted behind him.

"Hello, boy," the neighbor said blandly as she opened the door.

"H-hello," Papa stuttered. He paused a moment and tried to concentrate so the simple request would not take him a long time to say. "H-hello," he stuttered again. "M-m-my Ma want know if she can borrow sugar." He wiped his forehead when he was finished.

"What is that?" the neighbor asked, repelled by the black dog that stood behind Papa, who turned around and shook his head at the dog.

"Go!" he said. "Go from here!" he pointed to the road where the stick lay. Nobody sat still.

"That's your dog?" the neighbor asked, inspecting the Labrador.

"Yeh. My Pa bring it home today," Papa said.

"Hm. What's his name?" she asked.

"N-Nobody."

"Nobody? Nobody is the dog's name?" she asked and shortly after burst out with laughter. "Well, that's something," she said finally after catching her breath and hissed her teeth. "Wait here," she said and disappeared from the front door into the house. She returned with a small jar of white sugar cubes and handed it to Papa.

"Thank you," he told her and left her front porch, where she stood and watched him until he left.

"Didn't I tell you to stay there?" Papa said out loud. Nobody followed him, and continued to sniff the road as he had done on the way to the neighbor's house. A car drove past them and honked as Nobody drifted to the middle of the street.

"Stay here!" Papa yelled to the dog, as it ran quickly back to his side from the flying rocks that sped through the tires of the speeding car.

Nobody stopped in the road as Papa continued to walk. At first he did not care and continued to walk along with the glass of sugar cubes back to his house. Then he turned around to find that the dog was still behind him sniffing the grass. From the house at the end of a bougainvillea garden, two boys approached. Before Papa could speak, the boys were taking turns throwing stones at Nobody and Papa ran toward them.

"Leave my dog!" Papa had said.

"And what you will do? Go back to the village and tell your country Ma?" one said and threw another stone.

"My Ma's not country," Papa said.

"Where is she then? That's not your Ma at your Pa's house. Why nobody seen your real Ma?"

And Papa could not answer. Even he did not remember her, only her promise that she would one day return for him after leaving him with his father.

"You country boy, say you country boy. Your Pa Congo, that don't mean you're not a heathen."

And this was my favorite part of the story. One of the stones the boy had thrown landed on Nobody's neck and he yelped. And Papa, when he saw this, grew ten feet tall, right where he stood. Nobody hid behind Papa, and he picked up those stones that had fallen and began to throw them back. One of them even flew into the window on the boys' house. And he knew he would get a beating that night because of it, but he did not care. He threw and threw, and he was so strong that the stone went into another window. And he was so strong, so tall, that he picked those bullies up, one at a time, and he threw them across the yard. And he was so strong that one of the stones he threw, the heaviest one, landed on one bully's shirt and pinned him to the ground. It took days and three whole men to push it out of the way and free the bully. And from that day on, they never touched him or Nobody again. They stopped calling him names, stopped making fun of him for being only half of his father, and they barely even looked his way when they returned to school.

While we traveled through the checkpoints to Junde, I remembered, though he looked quite different and skinnier now than he was in Caldwell, that Papa had the incredible power to transform into a giant who could protect us and carry us away.

The third-to-last checkpoint was set up in the middle of a road beside an abandoned store. There were tables outside the store where guns lolled on top of one another. One soldier sat next to the table with guns while he cleaned the one in his hand with a torn and dirty camouflage cloth. Across from the building, there was a tank that some of the dragon's men leaned against and sat on. The remaining soldiers crowded the road and questioned each group and individual traveler about who they were, what tribe they were from, where they were going, what they did for a living, if they knew anything about the war, or if they were on the side of the prince of the rebels. When the soldiers stopped us to ask questions, I saw the fear lift from Papa's eyes as he transformed into the giant that I knew and loved.

"Stand and be recognized," they would say.

Papa stepped forward.

"What your name? Where you from? You Gio?" a soldier asked him.

"Augustus Moore. Monrovia," he answered and Ol' Ma squeezed my shoulder.

"You people Congo? You Congo man?" the soldier said as his eyes scoured our small group for signs. The soldier's eyes rested on Ma, who wore a lappa like she had just come from the country, and he looked quickly back at Papa.

"You Congo man?" he asked again as Papa avoided his eyes. "Where you work?"

"At the university," Papa answered.

"You got ID with you?" the soldier asked.

"In my bag, yeh," Papa said and Torma handed him the backpack she carried. Papa handed the soldier an identification card, and he looked like he did not believe whatever the card said, and he kept looking at Papa to make sure the man on the card was the man in front of him.

"Go," the soldier said, and we walked past him and joined the rest of the crowd toward the north.

We followed him. Sure that, like all giants, he had the ability to see an end of the road that we could not. I was small, and if I had any power like him, I was no more than a fairy whose hand barely fit into his palm. I left all of my dust in a small teacup in my room corner in Caldwell, so the only power I had to share with him was the power of touch, something that my sisters and I perfected one afternoon as we held hands and flew from our back porch with old lappas tied like capes to our backs. So I touched the leg of his pants as he walked.

"You all all right?" he asked.

"Yeh," I answered, and did not let go of his pants until the next checkpoint, where Torma took my hand as Papa moved forward to speak to the soldiers.

"Stand and be recognized," they said. We had just passed a Gola man who lay on the ground sleeping, and Papa stood in line to be questioned while Ma took us ahead to pass the checkpoint. Papa was Gola and Congo, and from Arthington, just like Taylor, so what if the soldiers thought he was like one of the prince's people and wanted to get rid of Hawa Undu?

Once again he became the giant. The dragon's men asked the same questions about who he was and where we were headed. The soldiers questioned Brother James and Amos just as thoroughly. Brother James stuttered as he answered the questions, but the soldiers let them all pass down the road walled by flowers with blackened petals.

When we continued, I ran to Papa's side and continued to hold on to his legs. My power was minimal, but maybe it would be what he needed, if the soldiers came for us, to gather me and the rest of his fairies, Wi and K, and Torma, too, and Ma and Brother James and Amos. Perhaps it would help him, if only small small, but still, to gather us together and hold us over his shoulder until we laughed ourselves into disappearance and rest, fufu dinner and so much Tang powder that our tongues remained orange for days after.

Amos decided that he would try his luck east into Ivory Coast and then Ghana, and he parted ways with us after the second checkpoint. He walked into Papa's chest and thanked him, crying like a spanked child.

"I will pray for y'all," Amos said as tears plunged to the ground from his face. "I owe you."

"Do not worry, Amos. We will be back soon. This thing will finish soon, yeh?" Papa said.

"Yeh," Amos answered slowly.

By the final checkpoint I had barely any more power to give to the giant; however, I stayed close to his side. We had not eaten all day, because the giant wanted to make sure that we reached Junde by night, so as my stomach twisted with hunger I squeezed the giant's pants to give him all of the juice that I had left in me.

Again, Torma took my hand as the giant approached the men.

"Stand and be recognized," they said. Papa stepped forward.

"Where you people from?" I heard a soldier ask him. Another soldier nodded at Ma and she pushed our backs to walk ahead to the end of the checkpoint. The same man pointed at Brother James to stand in line with Papa and continued to sort through the escapers. Papa's university card had worked so far, and as we moved to the front of the line to cross the checkpoint Ma turned around and stopped so that we could wait for him to pass with us across the final checkpoint.

The giant was taking longer than during the previous checkpoints, and as he spoke to the soldier the man's nostrils flared and he beckoned more soldiers to come to him. Brother James was cleared and nearly jogged toward us.

"What's wrong?" Brother James asked when he reached us and noticed Ma's distressed face.

"The people still asking him questions," she murmured.

There were three soldiers around Papa now. One of them yelled at the other one and touched the trigger and head of his rifle in front of him.

"Come," Brother James said and we returned to where Papa stood.

Before we reached him, one of the dragon's men took Papa's arm and pushed him toward a line on the side of the road where men stood with their hands behind their backs and looked out onto the road, looked down to the ground with what looked like water around their eyes, or knelt on the ground with folded hands, screaming things like:

"Please-oh! I hold your foot!"

And not too far from the line to which they pushed Papa, there were men lying on the ground. How could they sleep at a time like this? Didn't they know the giant needed them?

"But my daughters!" Papa said. The soldier continued to push Papa while another pointed the nose of the gun at his head, the air boiling around him.

"Take them to the booth," another said when he noticed us.

"You all hurry," he said underneath his breath as we all entered the booth on the side of the road, a small room with a window that faced where Papa and the other men stood.

"What's happening? Where's Papa?" Wi asked before looking out of the window to find Papa among the men waiting in the line.

The men in the line were other Gola and Congo men, someone passing said. During wartime, a man will not only find the person he hates to kill him, but he will find and kill anyone whom he thinks the person he hates loves or knows or once did business with. Papa looked at Ma from outside the window.

"Ay-man!" Brother James said, slapping the wall of the booth. He leaned against the wall and buried his face in his hand.

"What we can do?" Ma asked as she tapped his arm.

"Nothing-oh," he murmured.

"What Papa doing?" Wi asked Ma again.

Ma sat on a small stool in the corner of the booth and while rocking back and forth, she raised her hands into the air and shouted questions to God. Torma attempted to pull us away from the window.

"No," Wi said, pushing her hand.

I tapped the window in hopes of getting the giant's attention. He glanced at me, not as though he was happy to see me, but as though I was doing something wrong and he wanted me to stop. I continued and was joined by my sisters. He was a giant and I knew that he would be able to rescue himself from that line and rescue us from that box on the road. Torma stepped away from us and leaned beside Brother James against the wall; she held herself and sniveled softly. I was a "big geh" now with no hand on my back to soothe me as Papa's face grew pitch black in the last of the golden sun. The soldiers who were not questioning other escapers paced in front of the booth as my sisters and I continued tapping. The giant looked out onto the road.

Wi started crying first, and I wanted to be stronger for my family in the booth, and my hero outside, but I cried as well and with both of my palms I beat on the window of the booth with my sisters. K followed our lead, although she walked back and forth from the window to Ma's side, where Ma continued to pray, ignoring my small sister's plea for attention and reassurance.

"Papa! What Papa doing?" Wi screamed through a fury of tears and spit as she pounded the window. We pounded. We beat to overpower the drums. The guns. We pounded.

"Papa, come let's go!" I shouted, wanting him to fly to us and gather us up in his arms.

A passing soldier came to the door of the booth, angry as his jaw fell to reveal crooked yellow teeth.

"Shut them up!" he shouted. Disrupted from her prayer, Ma came to get us away from the window; but we all fought to remain, pushed her hand and chest as she attempted to pull us away.

"Shut them up!" the soldier shouted again.

"Children," Ma said softly first, before her voice escalated in fear. "Shh! Children!" but we pushed and kicked to stay near the window in close sight of Papa.

Our misbehavior in the booth nearly tipped it over and the passing crowd was delayed when they noticed the noise coming from it. Brother James tried to hold us down also, but he was pushed away like Ma and Torma.

After waiting at the opening of the booth for us, and on several occasions grabbing his gun as if he was going to shoot us to sleep, the soldier left the opening of the booth and walked to where Papa stood. He pulled him from the line and asked him more questions. After a couple of minutes he pulled the giant's arm toward the booth where we wrestled with Ma and Brother James. The soldier pushed Papa's back and returned to a group of other armed guards. Surprised and trembling, the giant stumbled to the opening of the booth, where we ran to him crying. I wrapped my arm around his leg and squeezed.

"Go, go, go," he said and we nearly fell over each other's feet across the line to Junde, all astounded, all grateful, none looking back.

That night as we slept, waiting for the canoe that would carry us along a still river to Lai, I lay against the giant's chest. Rebels had not seized Junde. It was still one of the dragon's cities, they had said. In

Junde, Papa found a fisherman who agreed to take us to the village in the forest, where we would sail the unstirred waters, where we would walk briefly through the woods until we reached a circle of houses, hidden from the war outside. I unfolded Papa's hands and pressed mine against his palms in the last house on our journey from Caldwell. There were many families asleep there that night, some hoping to make it all the way to Sierra Leone, some planning to stay in Junde until the fighting in Monrovia stopped. I asked Papa to sing to us, and he did. K and Wi lay near Ma, and Torma lay across from them as she played with the stem of a pink flower that had only one petal left.

NINE

Lai was our hiding place. Mam had told us many stories about her visits there when she was a small girl. The rooster and the sun fought, each morning, over which one would welcome the day. The hum of Lake Piso was a part of every conversation, both during the day and in our dreams. The houses in the village formed a circle around a sandy plot of land, where the villagers frequently met. There were two large orange trees in the corner of the village, close to the lake, Piso, that flowed back to Junde. Behind the houses were woods, full of cotton and kola and ironwood trees, that had to be crossed in order to get to a vast forest, and if you walked that forest for long enough you would reach the Atlantic Ocean, which Vai legend claims was the same beach where old Vai kings did business with German and Portuguese people. When we got to Lai, we saw that Mam's family from the city was already hiding there. My cousin Cholly was Papa's roommate. And Ol' Pa Charles, Mam's father, a man so tall he made Papa look like his son when he stood beside him, and who always patted my head when he passed me. Torma was home in Lai now, and she joined her family and lived across the village in another house.

On July 29, 1990, a group of boys dressed as Hawa Undu's soldiers went into St. Peter's Lutheran Church, where six hundred civilians were hiding. It was two in the morning. When the first shot was fired, those who were hiding quickly arose from the bare floors where they slept and scrambled for an escape from the compound. But as the lanterns were lit in the dark, they found Hawa Undu's soldiers surrounded them; all the men, women, and children were attacked with guns, grenades, and swinging machetes. On the following day the remains of the six hundred were paraded along the streets and burned. Hawa Undu decided on that day to speak to the BBC.

"I will not step down!" President Doe said. "It was rebels dressed in army uniforms that killed the civilians at the church. Charles Taylor's men did it. Not army soldiers. Rebels killed them. But no rebel can kill me. Only God can."

The BBC also said that 375,000 Liberians were now in Ivory Coast, Guinea, and Sierra Leone.

The voice from the small radio was muffled, but loud enough for the small group of men surrounding it to hear. They set the radio on the window of a tiny wooden chicken coop. One of the men stood near the radio and held the edge of the antenna between two of his fingers, twisting it periodically for improved reception. Papa was with them, sitting on a plastic stool close to the outside walls of the broken-down shack. And he looked like he was trying to make a serious face, the kind of face someone makes to hide something serious. Only a few of the men had spent enough time outside of Lai and bordering towns to know English well. Most only spoke Vai, but they crowded around the radio because every other man in the village was doing so. When the man on the radio paused, one of the villagers repeated what he said in Vai. Papa kept his journal with him, a leather-bound book now worn to shreds. While sitting with these men, Papa wrote down words and phrases they were saying. He asked questions when he did not recognize a word, and the villagers took turns telling him the answer.

In the mornings, the front door swung and the smell and sound of the lake rushed to our resting bodies, while Ma laid a mat on the front porch. The rooster from the coop crowed, and she knelt down on the mat and lowered her head several times, murmuring phrases to herself that I did not understand. Ma boiled a small pot of water from Piso and set it on the porch to cool before we rose. We changed into dresses that Pa had recently sewn for us from cloth the villagers gave him, and we joined hands and ran across the village circle to where Papa had already risen and was reading, waiting for us to join him. The girls and I climbed a lumber ladder to his loft.

On those mornings, Papa tutored us in what he had learned, the new words of the small village. We were quizzed on the meanings of words and he made us talk to each other in Vai. The process left me bitter when Papa shook his finger at me for creating words he called foolish and unserious. After our Vai lesson we were given math problems, simple addition and subtraction that we completed with stones he collected from the outskirts of the village.

After we completed our lessons we returned to Ma's house, where we ate small cups of white rice with her and took turns telling her about our morning lessons.

"Ay-yah," Ma would say, laughing and touching our faces and cheeks like Mam would. Ma was regaining her strength and weight back from the weeks we spent walking, when she had been reduced to merely skin, bones, and a faint wheeze as she struggled for breath in the sun. Lai was where she was raised, and where Mam was raised before her family moved to the city, the daughter, granddaughter, and great-granddaughter of Vai chiefs whose graves sat at the edge of the village toward the woods for everyone to see.

"Go now," she said after we were finished eating. "Play," she said, urging us to join the other children in the circle.

"Yeh, go." Pa playfully swatted us out of Ma's house. "Go meet the other children."

We could not fully understand what the children were saying, or they us, so we wanted little to do with them. Our favorite place to gather was between the orange trees, where we had a clear view of the village children as they played in the circle. They chased each other, busied themselves with hand games to which they sang along in Vai, and ran in and out of the houses. They had lived in Lai their entire lives.

While playing, Wi gathered the spoiled oranges left scattered underneath the tree and with them made a circle that surrounded us. When the circle was complete, mud and weeds rested between Wi's fingers and she came to where K and I sat in the middle with sticks.

"What is this?" Wi asked, drawing two circles attached to one another by a crooked line.

"What is this?" K asked after studying Wi's drawing and emulating the exact same thing in the dirt.

"That's the same thing I drew!" Wi said, annoyed and offended.

"No it's not," K argued.

"Both of them *jah-oe*," I said laughing, pleased that I had found a way to use the word I had recently learned meant "ugly."

"*Jah-oe, jah-oe,* drawing *jah-oe*," I teased them until Wi pushed me. I continued laughing at her nonetheless. A village girl ran to us from the circle across the village where the other children played. She watched us carefully first; she smiled at the fun I sounded and looked like I was having.

"Hello," the girl said, pulling the strap of her dress up her arm and over her shoulder. She was barefoot and her hair was parted into small cornrows, like ours. We looked up at her but continued what we were doing—Wi pushing me, me dodging her pushes, and K smiling at what she genuinely believed was her original artwork.

"Hello," the girl said again. Wi met the girl at the margin of our orange circle.

"You speak English?" Wi asked. The girl covered her mouth with her hands as she laughed and looked down at the ground.

"Hello," the girl said again.

"*Jah-oe*," I shouted at her. I rolled over in the dirt, overcome with laughter. At first she looked surprised, but the girl then covered her mouth with her hand and laughed. Wi laughed also, then walked over to me and pulled me up from the dirt.

"Stop, you will get dirty," she said. I sat up, still showing my teeth.

"*Y beh may-wah manna?*" the girl asked.

She wanted to know what we were doing. I giggled. I understood her.

"Drawing," Wi answered her.

The girl looked down at the broken sticks and pointed at the images in the dirt. "Drawing," she said. Wi met the girl at the edge of the circle, took her hand, and led her inside the circle of old fruit where K and I sat. K dropped the stick in her hand and ran out of the circle toward the house where Papa lived.

"Drawing," the girl said again, as she picked up the stick that K dropped and added shapes of her own.

"*Yhen,*" she said. "Drawing. *Yhen.*"

"*Yhen,*" Wi and I said together.

Ajala was the daughter of a Lake Piso fisherman. She said Vai words quickly, and we laughed at the way the words sounded. When the other children saw us play with Ajala, they came to the orange trees, until eventually the orange circle was full of children dodging thrown English and Vai words while drawing in the dirt.

From a distance, K approached us with Papa. He walked quickly toward the circle and it looked like he thought something had happened to me or Wi. When they reached us, Papa peered down at K, who pointed into the circle at Ajala.

"She asked what we were doing," she said to him, out of breath from the trouble she had gone through to find him. "She asked what we were doing in Vai."

In August, in our third month in Lai during the rainy season, Wi and I woke up one day to go attend our lessons with Papa. K did not. On either side of her, Wi and I shook her tiny arms and pulled our hands back from her skin as our palms dripped with her sweat. I wiped the fluid on the mattress and looked at her as she lay still, only slightly moving her head and moaning. Her hair was soaked and her dress clung to her skin, showing her gaunt legs and waist. Something was wrong. Water trailed down her face and arms, her legs, and through the thin dress she was wearing. Her lips shivered. She shouted, even though her eyes were closed. Some English words. Some Vai words. For Mam. Things that did not make sense. The shouts widened and her sentences rambled on.

"Ma!" Wi yelled out.

"Ma!" she said, running to the door as Ma rushed in.

"What's wrong?" Ma asked, kneeling down beside the mattress when she noticed K trembling on the wet sheet.

"She won't wake up," Wi answered.

Ol' Ma unfolded her head tie and used the cloth to wipe K's body. In days past, K had become whiny, constantly vomiting the rice and seafood that she was fed (all that we ever ate), and she wanted to sit in Papa's or Ma's lap instead of playing. We were used to her shadow behind us, or pressing her ear against a whisper that was only intended for Wi and me and getting pushed away—but she had no desire to mimic us that rainy season, she had no need of our secrets.

"Go get your papa," Ma said, still wiping K's body and patting her face.

"Papa!" Wi yelled. "Papa!"

We heard movement in some of the other houses as villagers came to their doors and windows to see who and what was causing the commotion. Some looked scared that the drums had found our hiding place.

"Papa!" Wi yelled.

When we reached his house across the circle, Papa had already made it out of his front door.

"What happened?" he asked.

"K won't wake up," Wi said. Papa ran ahead to Ma's house and we followed him. Several villagers who had woken up from our yelling followed us to Ma's house, where K still lay in a pool of sweat across Ma's arms. K's body shook, and she kept saying those foolish things, one after the other, eyes closed tightly. Papa knelt beside her and took her from Ma. As a crowd gathered outside, an elderly man pushed through the villagers and into Ma's house.

"What happened to the girl?" he asked Ma in Vai.

"It looks like malaria," Ma cried to the man, exasperated.

The man walked to where they sat with K. He went back outside where he told a few others to prepare a large bucket of warm water and *jollobo* leaves to bathe her in.

"What's going on?" Papa asked Ma.

"They want to bathe her in *jollobo*. It will lower her fever."

"No. No country medicine."

"Gus, please."

Papa held K tightly as her tears and sweat saturated the surface of his shirt.

"Gus, please. At least it will lower her fever," Ma said, attempting again to take K out of his arms.

Papa refused again as he gently wiped her face. He stood up, cradling her wet and trembling body, and walked outside and through the crowd to the back of the house, where several men and women poured boiling water from a rice pot into a tub of water from the village well. They then dropped *jollobo* leaves, each twice the size of their faces, into the large tub of water. Wi and I followed him as he moved toward it. The villagers surrounded the *jollobo* bath, and Papa, now trembling himself as K continued to melt in his arms, knelt down in front of it. Two women knelt down beside Papa, but he shook his head and blocked their hands.

"I will do it," Papa said with a breaking voice. He peeled the thin white dress over her head, taking care. Her sweat became his, and he held K's body over the tub of floating leaves. He lowered her into the water until her legs hid underneath the dark green plants.

"Lay her down to her neck," Ma said, kneeling beside Papa. She dropped her hands into the water and cupped her palms for a small amount that she sprinkled over K's head and hair. Ma did this several times, stroking K's hair. She then took a leaf from the bath and rubbed it against my sister's arms and legs until the water turned too cold for them to keep her in it.

"Where?" I heard Ma ask in a loud voice.

"Junde. I already asked the fishermen to use the boat," Papa insisted. "I just came to tell you. I'm going."

"What? If you go, the people will kill you. You hear the radio. It's worse out there now," Ma said, following Papa to his house across the circle. "They almost killed you coming."

"She's been sick for one week. If I don't go—" He stopped. K still was not eating and every night she screamed those rambling sentences as the family gathered in Ma's house and watched her sleep. Wi and I stayed by K's bed, sorry now for pushing her away. Her body lay still except for the times she was screaming, and many visited her bedside during the week to offer prayers and good wishes as she slept.

"Gus, please," Ma pleaded with him as he gathered a shirt and shoes from his bed and placed them in his backpack. He climbed back down his ladder to where Ma still stood, now crying.

"There was a clinic I saw while we were in Junde. Maybe I can find something there," Papa said, walking out of his house and back across the village circle.

"You scared. I scared too. All these people, everybody scared. But you can't go back in war," she yelled after him.

"She needs antibiotics, Ma," he argued.

He approached Ma's house, where Wi and I sat on the porch, watchers of K's body.

"Papa's going away for small, yeh?" he said into my eyes. "I'm going to find medicine for K."

Wi nodded.

"Listen to what Ma says, yeh?" he said.

"How long?" Wi asked.

"For small small," he said. I ran inside the house, where K lay asleep. I fought through the thick smell of her sickness for my slippers. I looked near the door, where they usually sat in a pile beside Ma's prayer mat. When I did not see them there or anywhere on the floor, I searched the porch.

"What you looking for?" Ma asked me, but I did not respond since all of my attention was required for the hunt. When I did not find them there, I ran around Ma's house and searched the ground for them, almost bursting into tears, at the time lost in my pursuit. It was then I remembered that the last time that I had seen them they were near the mattress where K slept. I hurried back inside the house and knelt beside the mattress. I crawled around it until finally I saw the backs of my slippers protruding from underneath the mattress. I grabbed the shoes and put them on, flustered that I had taken so long to find them. I ran out of the house and off the porch.

"Tutu! Where you going?" Ma yelled behind me as I dashed through the village circle toward Piso.

"Tutu!" she called, running after me. At the edge of the village I pushed through the bushes, scraping my arms on sharp, loose branches.

"Tutu!" Ma yelled and I heard multiple footsteps behind me. Still I continued toward the shore of the lake. I pushed the last shrub out of my way and ran to the shore, where in the distance Papa floated in a canoe along the still water toward Junde.

"Wait!" I said waving my arms. "Wait!"

Papa looked up and made a face so that even from a distance I could tell he was not pleased. Ma and Pa reached me, panting together from the long run.

"Wait!" I said once more, stomping my feet on the shore until the sand jumped and stained my shins and knees. Ma touched my shoulder to turn me around and I collapsed against her, while Papa yelled something at me that sounded like what Mam said before she left. "I will be back."

TEN

Ol' Pa saved all of his words for the times he knew it would matter the most, when after a question was asked everyone in the room became silent and their gaze floated toward the ceiling and sky. Otherwise he remained quiet—watched people as they spoke loudly and laughed with each other. Even sitting, he seemed taller than all of the other men in the village. He sat with his hands folded in his lap and listened to war commentary in both Vai and English, from Papa and the other men in Lai. A few days after Papa left, when it was still dark outside, I was shaken awake by Ol' Ma. She did not have to say anything. I knew what it was. I ran out of her house to the edge of the village where Papa stood, and I hugged him until my arms hurt. He looked so tired, but he had come back.

"I told you," he said while I cried. "I will never leave you for too long."

After Papa successfully returned from Junde with medicine for K, which completely healed her, he and other men made trips out of the village to retrieve food and other things from abandoned stores and houses in the small town.

Pa had made one trip before with Papa, after we ran out of food and Papa believed that it was the seafood from Lake Piso that was making us sick.

On this trip Pa planned on going to Burma, where he said he could find supplies, many in the same place, so Papa would not have to continue going in and out of the village when we had needs. Pa came into Ol' Ma's house one August morning as we sat with her for our sewing lesson. They brought back strips of cloth from a recent trip, and the girls and I took turns with Ma's spare needle, making what we decided would be a dress for Mam.

"Look," K said to him, showing the stitch she had just made in the arm of the garment. Pa inspected it and handed it back to her.

"Very good," he said to her. Ma noticed a burlap sack on his back and touched it to see if it was full.

"What you doing with that empty bag?" she asked.

"Going to Burma to find more food for the children," Pa answered.

"Burma?" Ma asked. "What's in Burma?"

"I will get more things than in Junde. I will come back soon," he said and the lines in his forehead sunk as he explained.

"Who's going with you?" Ma asked, standing up with him.

"Nobody. I will not be gone long. It will be better to go alone," he said. "People see you walking in group they will think you rebel."

Ma nodded, but she looked like she did before Papa left on a trip outside the village. He kissed her face as I had seen Papa kiss my mother.

He then knelt back down in front of us and stretched out his hands for us to hug him.

"What you want me bring back for you?" he asked us with serious eyes.

"Peanuts. I want some peanuts," I answered.

"You girls want peanuts?" he asked. My sisters agreed.

"Okay, my geh. I will bring your peanuts."

He stood up with the burlap sack hanging from his back and walked out of Ma's house to Lake Piso. He turned around and his wrinkled skin creased as he looked at Ma, and he waved. We watched him disappear behind the bushes that covered the lake.

"Come now, you girls. Come finish your dress," Ma said, pulling us back into her house.

We sat in front of the dress with zigzagging stitches across the front.

"It's a pretty dress," K said, caressing the cloth in Wi's hands.

"Mam will like it," K said to Ma.

"Yeh, she will like it plenty," Ma said. I grew excited at the memory of Mam's face and how it would wash over with joy when she saw the dress.

"Where is Mam?" K asked Ma.

"Mam still in America," she said.

"When is she coming back?" K asked, biting her lip as she looked up at the ceiling and followed it back down to Ma's face.

"Soon. She will be back soon and we will all go back to Caldwell. Yeh?" Ma said, trying hard to maintain a straight voice and face. K looked down at the dress in Wi's lap. She had stopped stitching and we were all looking up at Ma for an answer. Ma continued to sew, periodically looking in the corner at her prayer mat, mindful of the time.

On the following night a barefoot fisherman walked to Ma's porch where she sat plaiting Wi's hair.

"Hello, Ol' Ma," he said. "You know when Ol' Pa coming back? He took my boat." Papa walked up behind the man with a lantern in his hand. He came to read to us and wish us goodnight, as he did every night before we slept.

"I'm sorry," she said.

"What's wrong?" Papa asked Ma.

"The man is asking for Pa," she answered. "He will come back soon. He should have come this morning," she told the fisherman.

"Yeh, if he is not back by tomorrow night, we will send some boys to go look for him," Papa said, and it was clear he wished he had gone with Pa on this trip. The fisherman nodded and left the house.

"Pa coming tomorrow?" I asked.

"Yeh," Ma said, wiping her face. She squeezed the lappa and settled on the floor where we sat. She looked into our faces as though they were road maps back to her love; she inquired silently and glanced about the wooden walls of her small house. He was neither there nor in our faces, not on the village circle or near the coop.

"Don't worry, Ma. We will go look for him tomorrow," Papa said. Ma untied the head tie from her head and cried into the aloe-scented cloth as her thick black hair fell to her back.

She met Pa when she was a teenager, they said, in those days when she could finally walk to the market in the evenings while her younger sisters and brothers continued working on the farm. The Vai people had been in Cape Mount for hundreds of years then. Pa was at a market stand selling the garments he'd sewn, the most crowded stand since he was so tall that it was hard to miss him. Ma had passed him while holding a friend's hand, they said. They made sure their hair was fully covered as they approached him. He saw her pass and pointed directly at her.

"You," he said with a voice as tall as him. "You will be mine."

"But wait," she answered in Vai. "Don't I have a choice?"

Ma giggled and ran away with her friend. Some days later when she returned home from the farm, Pa was waiting there talking to her parents.

"He says he loves you. He says he wants you," her Ma had said as she pulled her out of the room. "Do you want him? Do you love him?"

She had not seen him since the day she met him at the market.

Ma peeked into the room as Pa sat with his hands on his knees, nodding as her father questioned him. Her father was a chief, and she knew that the business of her marriage was a serious one. But there was this big, tall man, handsome, brave, and special even, she had said.

"Yes," she said quickly.

Pa was made to convert to Islam to take Ol' Ma's hand in marriage. They had eight daughters and one son, three children dying before ten years old. Pa moved with her, almost right away, from Ma's village. Ma's father had not sent any of his daughters to school. The women were supposed to work on the farm with their many children while the men sat underneath palaver huts with their neighbors to discuss politics.

"I do not want a family on a farm," he had told Ma when she became pregnant with her first daughter. And against Mam's grandfather's wishes, Pa took his children to the nuns at Catholic schools in Sierra Leone and Liberia, begging them to see his daughters through. As they grew, they would travel to London and France, to America and across Africa to "learn book." The Ol' Ma had educated daughters—something in her old age she was most proud of—a mold finally broken by that big man she knew at once she loved. He had changed her, as great loves do. And she had changed him—his only wife, his princess. And where was he now? How could he leave her now?

The next morning Papa left with a cousin and two other villagers in a canoe headed for Junde. The entire village knew now of Pa's disappearance and they stood on the shore of the lake to bid Papa and his cousin a safe journey. Through the traffic of villagers, as I stood underneath Ma's hand, I thought of Pa's shoulders and how they turned toward us on the day he left. It was my peanuts that he went to find, a simple wish I wanted to take back, and begged God that Ma would not remember. When day broke again, a woman near the lake yelled out for Ma. With her head unwrapped, something that I rarely saw her do, she rushed out of her house and across the village circle to the lake, where a canoe came toward her in the water. Some villagers woke up when they heard the yelling woman and followed Ma into the clearing, holding their lappas as they ran onto the shore. But the same number of men who had left on the previous day returned, fatigued and distressed by the unsuccessful search. Ma looked like she was still looking for someone else in the canoe, long after the last man stepped onto shore. The hands of villagers covered her back and shoulders. They gave water and a helping hand to Papa and the other men who were in the canoe. When Papa reached her, Ma fell into his arms, almost throwing him over with her grief.

"Nah-mah," Papa said, pressing her head into his chest as he held her up. "He will come back," he said, although he did not look Ma in the eyes. And after he hugged us, he did not look me in the eyes either. Several times during that day, Ma stood up from her porch and looked across the circle to the lake. She walked across the village, past the shrubs that blocked her view, and waited on the shore of the lake for Pa. While watching her, still hoping that she did not remember what I told Pa before he left us, I thought of Mam and wondered if we made her this sad. I wondered if she was walking to the edge of her America and looking across the ocean for a ship that had us in tow, if she was crying, if she wanted us as much as Ma wanted and waited for Pa.

At dawn everyone in the village was awake. The men stood near the radio by the chicken coop, talking about whether or not to send another group to look for Pa if the most recent search came back without him. The women took turns bringing Ma soup and begging her to eat, because for the past week she had sat on her porch crying, and sometimes she even sounded like K did when she had malaria. The children were told not to run around the circle and that we should be mindful that Ma was sick and instead play quietly inside our houses. My sisters and I passed the time by her side.

In front of the lake, a bush shook, and Ma quickly stood up on the porch. The company of men had returned from the search, and when Papa saw them he rushed to them from where he sat near the radio. Before he arrived where the three men stood, one of them, a boy, took his shirt off and ran into the village circle.

"THE OL' PA DEAD! CHARLES FREEMAN IS DEAD!" he cried before he fell in the middle of the circle, collecting his shirt in between his fingers and burying his face in it. Charles Freeman. That was Ol' Pa's name. My heart shook between its walls. Villagers ran out of their houses, and when they saw the boy in the middle of the circle, they started stomping the ground with their feet and yelling with their hands stretched out to God. Ma fainted onto her porch. Papa ran across the circle, picked her up, and carried her limp body inside her house. A crowd rushed in, mothers and daughters and sisters, sons and uncles and cousins, friends. Papa laid her on the mattress, and Torma used a stiff piece of cardboard to fan her. There were so many people surrounding her that I was pushed to the doorway and could only catch sight of her between their busy bodies. I had heard of death in many forms. The kind where spirits joined ancestors and lingered around us. The kind where a person went to paradise and waited for God in heaven to call them up. The kind where a soul is taken by God to a life after the one on earth. None of these seemed to be ways of bringing his body back, of seeing him walk heavily through that clearing with all of us on his mind and a smile so we would know. My Ol' Pa was gone. I would never see his body again. I stood in the doorway, looking first at the crowd around Ol' Ma, then toward Lake Piso and its part in it all, and I knew. There was something wrong, deeply wrong, on the other side. There were no drums, no slumber. There was something deeper. Something else. There was no savior to restore a forest full of troubles, and I wanted Mam. I only wanted Mam.

"Wake up, Ol' Ma," an older woman said, patting Ma's face with dry hands. "Ol' Ma, wake up."

Ma's eyes gradually opened to a looming crowd of wet eyes. What had happened, what he said, what it meant, it looked like it all came to her at once, and she tore her dress from her body, spellbound. Standing at the door, I watched Ma throw her head tie to the floor as she frayed her hair with her fingers, and her heart escaped from her mouth.

ELEVEN

The rocks and stones in the forest are plenty, but none will make a sound when they are stepped on. And the skeletons in the forest are plenty, but none will break to make a sound when they are stepped on. And the crocodiles in forest swamps, they fuss plenty and snap and tease, but not even they make sounds when they are stepped on. They just swim deeper. They hide.

When a prince entered the forest, the monkeys were already silent. There were two then—Charles Taylor and Prince Johnson—and Johnson was the prince who entered first to kill Hawa Undu and restore Liberia. Johnson stepped on the plenty rocks and stones, stepped on the skulls and crocodiles and none made a sound. On September 9, 1990, the wind stood still among the leaves and a prince finally captured the dragon. Hawa Undu clawed and howled but his fire had left him. The prince did not want to kill the dragon in the forest, because he believed the forest would one day be his, so he dragged Hawa Undu to his own house by his tail while the dragon's teeth clapped, and he tied him with ropes made of shaven tree bark. The prince ripped off Hawa Undu's scales, one by one, while he begged for mercy. The prince's rebels surrounded Hawa Undu, spat on him, mocked him, made him howl, and praised the prince for fulfilling the promise he made of finally killing the dragon and ending this war.

The prince told them to beat Hawa Undu, and the rebels took their fists and clubs and beat Hawa Undu. He told them to cut his hands, which were guilty of stealing from the Liberian people, and the rebels cut his hands, one finger at a time. The prince told them to cut his ears because he did not listen when they told him to surrender on his own, and the rebels cut his ears. Hawa Undu would have at least tried to run away but they cut his toes, laughing while the ice from American beers chilled their throats. The rainy season was nearly gone so no thunder would drown out the sound of Hawa Undu dying. The powerful dragon who flew into a wall he denied was in front of him. Once a prince like his captor.

The prince dragged Hawa Undu's lifeless body through Monrovia's streets and left it there, bleeding from every opening. They said Liberia would be healed of her sickness after Doe was gone, that they had the pepper soup we needed. But these men who said they came to save Liberia, these men who say they come to save the world, they do not understand the curse of the forest. Those dreams of peace and noble rulers, they are gone. The trips to the market, the walks to the well, now ghosts among us. Those days of sweetness burned to ashes. Hawa Undu will never die. His spirit lives on, moves through the greed of those wretched heroes, all once princes, all once well-intentioned men.

By December 1990 the fighting had still not ended. The men in the village listened to a voice from the BBC on a rusty radio placed on a window's edge, and the latest was that Charles Taylor and Prince Johnson were now fighting each other for the presidential seat after Hawa Undu's death.

In Lai, we were not allowed to walk inside the chicken coop. It was more Papa's rule than any of the villagers' rule. Because Papa said this, we played around it. We opened the main trapdoor and waited for stray chickens and their babies to run out of their tin shack so that we could chase them. We hid outside the coop. Ajala pressed her finger to her lips and grabbed the edge of the shack door. We covered our mouths to keep from laughing. Ajala flung the door open and several chickens ran out, leaving tiny tiny footprints in the dirt. The young boys of the group scrambled to throw the chickens back into the coop.

"Look!" K said, pointing to the door where the orange chicken slowly came out. As it turned around to make its way back into the coop, Ajala shut the trapdoor, and the boys threw the remainder of the loose chickens through the window.

"*Pah, y nahla!*" Ajala shouted, pointing at a lone chicken. As if the chicken understood what Ajala said, it ran around the side of the shack. We followed, laughing as it managed to escape our clapping hands and waddled between our legs. We laughed as it led us around the coop twice, then through the cooking house, where the women sat over boiling pots of rice and stew. The chicken led us through the rice farm between the yellow stalks, where the farmers yelled at us to take the chicken back to the coop.

In the distance I heard a woman yell. When we heard that more than two women were yelling now, and saw in the distance some elders run toward their houses from the village circle, we stopped. The chicken clucked loudly and I searched the crowd of children for my sisters. Wi took our hands and we ran to Papa's house, where we were told to go at once if we suspected that anything was wrong. Villagers continued to run into their houses, and a crowd of men approached the opening to Piso, where a woman wore a camouflage vest and dragged a bottle of palm oil to the edge of the village circle. A gun hung on her shoulder, like the one the rebels carried on the road.

"They found us!" a villager shouted as she ran into her house, slamming the door. "I didn't come to start trouble," the stranger said to the crowd of men. "I'm looking for Gus Moore. Augustus Moore." Papa ran out of his house into the circle.

"Go into the house and close the door," he said to Wi.

Wi, like me, was unable to leave him, and after only a few steps she stopped and looked at the soldier woman from a distance.

"What is the problem here?!" Papa asked as he moved through the crowd of men and stopped when he saw the shiny gun on the woman's back.

"I'm looking for Augustus Moore. That's you?" she asked calmly.

"Yeh," Papa said. "What you doing here? How did you find us?!"

"I've come for you," she said, spitting on the ground in front of him. "You and your daughters."

"What do you mean you come for me?" he asked, raising his voice. "Who sent you?!" He sounded afraid, he thought he was shouting.

"Mam. Your wife," the rebel said and watched Papa's face change. He stood noiselessly. "Your wife come for you."

DRY
SEASON

TWELVE

Satta. I was still broken. I wanted a way out from thoughts of *him*, and Satta's memory came to me one night and stayed. It was a dream about her jug of palm oil, which she carried like a baby that day she came for us. I woke up and said her name in the dark, surprised to have remembered it all those years later. At that point I could not remember when last I had been outside. Some weeks prior I went to a store just below Eastern Parkway, one of the only stores of its kind that still existed among the deluge of coffee shops and yoga studios, to buy palm oil and frozen cassava leaf, to make the dish I knew would heal me, the only Liberian dish I made that tasted like Mam's. When I arrived, a sign informed me that the store had closed indefinitely, and, returning to my apartment, I felt everything I had been avoiding crashing hard into me, tears staining my skin. I have not been able to wash them off for some time.

Before moving there I rid the place of ghosts. I burned sage—the Ol' Mas say the spirits do not like the odor. I then called Mam and asked her to pray, certain they would listen to her voice, ascending in that musical way it did from my phone speaker, before they obeyed mine.

"I've been thinking about that woman," I told her that late fall.

"What woman?" Mam asked.

"The rebel. From the war. I dreamed about her."

"Oh," she said when the silence overstayed. "Have you spoken to K recently?"

"A couple days ago," I said.

"And you've eaten today?"

"I made cereal," I said. "Her name was Satta, right?"

"Yes," she said and breathed deeply into the phone. "You will be all right, Tutu."

And Mam made that sound of married curiosity and indifference, an impossibility, her best invention.

The five or so steps from my bed to the kitchen felt like uphill lunges. I spent too long looking into mirrors, too long sleeping, buried under covers still marked with our collective smell, every moment I was not working. I had made it to my living room that day and I opened the large window where I placed a vase of Mam's favorite flowers, lilies, now dried and unrecognizable in the escaping sun. The sill was cold when I climbed onto it, and I rested my slippers on the fire escape where children played below as we once did, and the Brooklyn drivers honked in the street while bits of conversations and laughter spilled from their car windows on the backs of words like *move* and *fell* and *going* and *tomorrow*, and the sirens came toward me from the distance, then disappeared again behind those words, and the new transplants hurried home, as gentrifiers do when it is almost dark and they are still fearful of corners.

I leaned my head against the stile and wondered how I smelled, how I looked, if music would ever sound the same, especially those songs I knew by heart. Wi called shortly after and I almost did not answer the phone because I did not care for the questions.

"How are you?" She asked this while exhaling, her daughters loud in the background.

"I'm fine," I answered.

"You getting your work done?"

"I am," I said, fighting the urge to look at my computer desk, the remote office where I spent a few hours a day consulting and freelance writing, then glaring into the orbit while an unedited novel sat idle on a minimized screen.

"Did you get out today?" She sighed again.

"I'm outside now," I mumbled, staring through the holes beneath my feet, three stories down to the ground below.

"Outside outside, or on your fire escape?"

I did not answer. So she said my name in that way only Mam would. Then there was that familiar litany of consolations, fumbling pauses and attempts to make me laugh, her optimism harsh against my ears. She reprimanded her girls every few minutes and if I were well I would have smiled. She was that good at it.

"I'll be fine," I said. "I just need time." And I needed my cassava leaf, the way they made it in Lai, spread over parboiled white rice drenched in oil, with shrimp, with dry fish and pepper that wounded my lips, reddened my skin, and those meats that required both hands to eat.

New York. By my midtwenties the transients around me were already collecting AA chips from too many weekends in Chelsea, habits that always felt unnatural to me because I have a low tolerance for pain and hangovers, and because the fundamentalist shadow of Mam and Papa's early Sunday mornings in Texas, even during my self-proclaimed late-teen rebellion, remained. My habit during those years was love stories. Grand, provoking, almost silly, intoxicating, appropriated from romantic comedies and Old Testament Scripture. I had fallen in love in that city and then out of it too many times to count. And so I fit in perfectly there, in that way wanderers like myself do in refined cities, where most wear love like loose garments.

But he stuck.

We had been together for two years, all of which were long distance. Long-distance relationships begin beautifully, end suddenly, sometimes by accident, and thereafter smoke rises not because all is burned to ashes but because there is always something left in the pipe.

This was the other side of love. Everything infuriated me, everyone was guilty. During the fall after that relationship, the days were long and mornings came too soon. The sun crept toward the body of that girl hidden under blankets, that girl still running, that girl who lay on bare floors with her Ol' Ma, who lay in New England attics with her new immigrant family, and that girl who lay with her sweetheart on an air mattress that flattened during the night, while he was in college or in med school or unemployed—in those days he could not afford a bed.

The Ol' Mas did not tell us that you could not throw away love once it was finished. That it would remain on us like blackened scars, underneath blouses and in those places only we could see. That we would reach a point where it, once solid, would melt in our hands and we would never fully wash off its residue; and that some love, the truest love, also the most dangerous, could disfigure our core.

I used freelancing as an excuse to make offices of Brooklyn cafés and city parks. An excuse to take spontaneous flights to visit my brothers and sisters in Texas after spending too many days pretending to understand the meaning of those paintings in Manhattan museums. An excuse to meet friends with nine-to-fives on thirsty Thursdays and giggle as they tried to stay awake at their desks the morning after, cursing me out with emojis via text, and thereafter promising them I'd make it up to them on the following week. Love was all around me, and yet once fall came, I barely left my apartment for reminders.

When we were children and the teachers told stories of love, we did not fully understand. Then they began to have different conversations with the girls than they had with the boys. They separated us into rooms in those elementary schools in Connecticut and in Memphis and in Spring divided by thin walls where we could still hear the boys laughing as they explained our parts, the unmentionable parts, the parts between our legs that were rude to speak of. And when we giggled our way through our questions, the teachers mentioned love, but we did not fully understand it. So Papa and Mam tried to explain it and they spoke of love in that creamy, sterilized way, stripped of those parts that were rude to speak of, and because they censored our parts, neglecting mention of those stiffening limbs, I did not believe its bigness. I ignored the rage in their eyes. "Our love for each other saved our family," they would say. "Our love for each other got us through the war," they would say. "My love for Mam," he said. "My love for Gus," she said. And how could anything I would find live up to that?

"Have you spoken to Mom and Dad?" Wi asked.

"I spoke to her this morning. Dad was at the university."

"I still can't believe they went back there," she said. "You sound better. A little better."

To this, nothing.

"Have you heard from him?" she continued.

"Every time I talk to Mam—"

"No," she interrupted. "Not Dad. I meant . . . well, sorry, never mind. I shouldn't have."

I pressed my bare feet against the cold bars of the fire escape. A cool breeze brushed against my face, separating the phone's mouth from mine.

"I've been thinking about that rebel. Who came for us," I said.

"What rebel?"

"During the war. It was weird. She was carrying palm oil like a little baby. In my dream. And I've had a couple of them."

"Hm," the sound came from my sister as half laughter, half disappointment. "Have you spoken to K?" she asked.

"Mom asked me that earlier. Is this an intervention?"

Wi laughed and I was better for it.

"Did you find someone?"

"I mean, I don't know. K becoming a shrink doesn't mean it's for everyone," I answered.

"She means well."

"Sure."

"It's just . . . it's just that none of us have seen you like this," Wi said. "You've had breakups, and I know this one was serious. And the dreams again. Mainly the dreams. I don't know. It's just . . ."

Nightmares were old friends. They started in Stratford. On that day, Mam made us wear three ill-fitting hooded black raincoats given to us by a member of our new church. She insisted that it would rain that day and we had no choice but to remain still as she pulled and tied the braided black strings so that the hoods hugged our chins. We were told to go to the bus stop holding hands, because although Connecticut traffic was nothing compared to what we had trekked through in Manhattan, Mam was convinced that the stillness of the Stratford town was more to be worried about than the taxis near Columbia's campus. The stroll was uncomfortable because as the pair of long johns underneath my jeans and sweater rode up, I could not reach my hand into my raincoat to pull them down (for fear that Mam was still standing at the front door watching until we boarded the bus, and would punish me if I let go of my sister's hand for too long). A honeybee stared at us when we arrived at the corner. Other than her peculiar shirt and pants, she wore black dress shoes with neon-yellow strings and a headband with two yellow cotton balls glued to the end of movable wire. A princess fairy joined her in ogling, raised her pink wand over her mouth as she whispered something to the bee with un-bridled giggles.

We were used to being on the receiving end of suspicious looks by then. Barely one year in and our new country let us know, every day, that we were different. As the children made their way to the bus stop, all sniggering and abnormally happier than the day before, they stopped and examined us with what appeared to be extraordinary disbelief and disappointment. When the bus pulled up at our corner, a Native American chief with red pillow feathers wedded to his head by a rubber band pointed toward my sisters and me and snickered. Wi pulled K's and my hands to the bus door and we followed her inside. We shared a seat in the front, two seats behind the driver. I reached into the arm of my raincoat and pulled the thermal down toward my wrist from the annoying bunch it had made underneath my armpit.

In my classroom, after taking off the dreadful raincoat, I was subject to the same attention my sisters and I received at the bus stop. Confounded as to why my classmates were still looking at me, even without the raincoat, I looked down at my shirt and inspected it for any stains. I made sure that my socks matched. I brushed the surface of my cornrows for food or lint that may have made beds there. A boy with two red horns jutting out from his head and a matching red bodysuit and tail rushed to my desk. I looked up at him from my seat.

"Who are you supposed to be?" he asked, his finger so close to my face that I could smell the potato chip crumbs stuck underneath his fingernails. I did not know what he was asking so I dropped my head and stared at my desk until he walked away. I had never seen any group of children as merry and energetic as the children in my classroom that day. I did not have any friends whom I could ask about what was so special about the day or why they were dressed foolishly, so I remained quiet at my seat in the corner of the room and eavesdropped on their fascinating conversations. As they spoke, I mimicked their words and intonations under my breath so that no one would hear me. After being consistently teased for my accent, I realized that I sounded as different to them as they sounded to me.

"Caaan-dy," I murmured, extending the first syllable like the girls in the front of the classroom. I laughed to myself at how it sounded.

When Ms. Proctor entered the classroom, two boys who wore matching blue capes and eye masks ran up and down the aisles parallel to my desk.

"Okay, settle down," Ms. Proctor said. "Sit down."

She was a pale old woman with a long neck and gray hair that she tied into a bun behind her head. She showed no interest in my difference. But on the annual teacher's day when our second grade class was allowed to bring gifts, when I nervously placed an apple on her desk (since I could not afford to buy her anything else) and I sat back down, I noticed that she was still smiling at me, in a way that only people who had told me they loved me had smiled at me before.

When the class was entirely seated, Ms. Proctor picked up a piece of chalk from the board and started to write something, but quickly erased it with her fingers. She wiped the chalk on her skirt and turned to face us with a smile.

"Okay. Who can tell me what today is?"

The lobster claws and superhero gloves waved in the air. I did not want to be the only student who did not have her hand raised, so following the lead of my classmates, I raised my hand as well.

"Oh, good. Yes?" Ms. Proctor pointed at me. My defeated classmates dropped their hands. At first Ms. Proctor smiled at the fact that my hand was actually raised, but after noticing the crestfallen look on my face, her face dropped and it was clear that she was sorry for her decision.

"Th-Thursday?" I answered, ashamed of the sound of my own voice, after a brief moment of silence.

Before I finished speaking, as expected, the entire second grade class fell back in their chairs in laughter. Some turned around and shook their heads at my obvious foreignness; others pointed and laughed until Ms. Proctor demanded that they get quiet again.

"Thursday?" one of the boys with a cape said, mimicking my accent. I was unaware that I sounded that way, and touched my lips while staring down at my desk.

"That's enough," Ms. Proctor said. "That's enough."

"I know," a fairy gloated in the front row.

"Good," Ms. Proctor said, wanting to get over the revelation. "What day is today?" She looked at the girl while rapidly batting her eyes.

"Halloween," the girl said, and as I lifted my head she was turned to face me and looked as if she would never need to win anything again.

Ms. Proctor wrote the word on the board as the class spelled it.

"Halloween," I murmured to myself and wondered if I sounded like them.

My sisters were also quiet on our bus ride home, so I imagined that we had all had similar experiences with our classmates. Mam stood on the front porch waiting, and at once we ran to her, impatient to share the news of the wondrous new day that had just entered our imaginations.

"It's Halloween!" we said simultaneously, almost immediately after reaching my aunty's yard. "It's Halloween!"

"Yeh, I know. Come inside," she said, holding the door open for us with a straight face.

"But—"

"Go wash your hands so you can eat, yeh? Then go to the basement for homework."

I felt betrayed and wanted to inquire further, but instead I walked up the hardwood steps opposite the front door to the attic where my family slept to drop off my things. We had only been there for a few months and every day I waited for Papa to return from those embassy lines, those employment lines, those immigration lines where he was ritually treated like a nonentity, to tell us, finally, that it was time to return to Caldwell. But that day never came, and our second home was in an aunty's Connecticut attic, an aunty who knew better than to stay in Liberia for as long as we did. We had two rooms facing each other. One for me and my sisters. One for Mam, Papa, and the baby.

We were told to be careful of stepping on the hand-tufted rug and discouraged from touching the glass windowpanes of our aunty's cherry armoires. Mam preferred that we not sit in the living room, for fear that we would leave food and finger stains that she would be too embarrassed to explain.

"Go get your book bags and go to the basement," Mam said as soon as we were finished swallowing the last of our snacks.

"Mam?" K said, standing up from the coffee table.

"Ask me after your homework, yeh? Go get your books and go to the basement."

I knew what K wanted to ask. Mam insisted on keeping a regular schedule, even though she knew what an incredible day it was. Fairies and bees and goblins all come to life. Princesses, toads, and tigers surrounded us that day, knew something we did not. My sisters headed for the attic to retrieve their bags, but I stayed and turned to face Mam at the doorway. I observed as she gathered our plates, laboring over the table. Still slender, still beautiful, with cheekbones that beckoned around corners. But changed. I thought of Torma and Korkor. Their promises that I would see Mam soon. That she would sing to me. That I would touch her again, hug her, sit in her lap. And how brief was that reunion. Where had she gone?

"What?" Mam asked, looking up from the stack of empty plates in her hand. "Go get your bag and go downstairs."

In the basement we were allowed to sit on the sofas and couches, although Mam preferred we do our work at the coffee table in the middle of them. She monitored our progress, quietly. The doorbell rang and Mam did not budge. She looked up at the ceiling and waited for the sound of keys. When the bell rang again, she shook her head and resumed the supervision of our home assignments.

"Doorbell," K said.

"Don't worry, yeh? Do your work," Mam said.

Shortly after, we heard a group of footsteps rush off of our aunty's lawn. Through a rectangular window adjacent to the ceiling, I saw a pair of striped socks and what looked like a black cape walk past.

"Pay attention to your work," Mam said.

"It's Halloween," K said for me, for all of us, finally. "They say *trick or treat* and dress up for candy!" The elucidation excited her.

"Pay attention, K. I know."

"Are we going to go for candy?" Wi asked.

"No," Mam said finally. "It's not a good day. Some things in this country are not good. The people dress their children like devils and witches and take them around to beg for candy," she said with a straight face. "It's not a good day."

In the bathtub that evening I instructed K to sit still while I covered her body with white soap foam. She laughed as I painted her body with the flattening suds and extended her arms out to either side of her so that I would not miss an inch.

"You can be a snowman for Halloween," I said.

Later on in our attic room, I sat on the windowsill and looked out onto the front yard. Wi and K were on the floor in front of a game of Chutes and Ladders, and as I waited my turn, I peered down at the passing fairytale characters and their counterparts. They carried plastic bags and buckets with illuminated pumpkin faces, all overflowing with candy and other treats. They hopped around with their parents, who looked just as content with the unruly and cheerful night. The darker it became, more children emerged from their homes with buckets of sweets—laughing and dancing in the street. I imagined myself down there—one hand touching theirs, rubbing its whiteness for the Africa underneath, the other tightly clenching my candy bucket. I thought then that perhaps my parents' understanding of this place, this America, was wrong. I doubt that they would have let us go outside and play with a horde of children all dressed as Gio devils in Liberia, but this place was different, and besides I would not have wanted to. But that night, I wanted to go outside. I wanted to walk with them; I wanted to exchange treats from their buckets, to sound and act and be like them, who seemed happier than I was, and at that moment happier than I would ever be.

"Papa's here!" K said, interrupting my daydream. Thrilled, I stepped down from the windowsill and ran down the attic steps to the living room, where I heard his voice.

"Papa!" I ran to him. He was slow to respond. Again.

Over time as I raced the girls to meet him at the door, he was slower to pick us up, and the kisses on our foreheads seemed lighter than the day before.

"Your daddy's tired, yeh," Mam would say as he moved through the living room as if weights constrained his heels and walked straight upstairs, saying less to us as days and nights took turns passing in our new country. His eyes were different—sometimes bloodshot and sunken, as his head slanted into his palm during deadlock daydreams toward the afternoon news. And his eyes, once a whisper of "It will be okay" or "Papa is right here" or another blend of words that persuaded our peace of mind, now seemed to say "We are lost" and "They do not want me here but we must stay" and "Papa is gone. I am sorry."

That night when Papa finally made it upstairs, all of the lights in the house were turned off except for those in the attic rooms.

"Okay, get in bed," Mam said, coming in first.

"Today is Halloween!" I shouted.

"Didn't I tell you girls already?" Mam said.

"I know," Papa interrupted. He placed K back on the bed beside me and kissed my forehead. By the time he made it over to Wi's bed to kiss her, Mam had already tucked us in under the covers and was shaking her head in disapproval.

"It's not a good day," he said finally.

My vision blurred with tears when he said this—because I knew that although America was new and different to them, by the way he said it, it was true.

"Why?" Wi asked.

"The people used to come out and worship devil long time ago," he said matter-of-factly. "It's not a good day."

"Okay, that's enough of this Halloween. Time to say prayers and sleep," Mam said.

I didn't want to speak to either one of them. When Papa was leaving the room, he turned around to me, sensing, I knew, the sadness of our exclusion from all things deemed normal and fun.

"I love you, yeh?" he said and disappeared in the darkness behind our closed door.

"Trick or treat," K giggled under the covers.

"Trick or treat," Wi repeated.

I closed my eyes to their muffled twitters until my body melted into the pink sheets and pillows. Their voices echoed in a dim and empty space until the laughter vanished and I stood on my bare feet on what felt like strewn pebbles. I took a step forward and I was back in Monrovia on a distorted dirt road with no end and infinite fields of yellow grass on either side. To the right of me, my father stood with his arms crossed and looked angrily ahead of us. He wore a torn shirt with mud and blood stains, and his body was reduced to a flesh-colored skeleton whose joints prodded from underneath his skin when he moved too sharply in one direction.

"Come," he said and took my hand. His shoes were backward on his feet and like slippers they slapped the road as we walked.

"Papa, where we going?" I asked.

He did not look down or respond. His pulled me with one hand and swung the other.

"Come," he repeated and squeezed my hand so hard that I felt it in my head.

"Papa, you're hurting me," I whimpered.

"Come," he said again, still refusing to look down at my face.

"Please, can we stop?"

A wooden house with a broken front door appeared ahead on our right. A figure that I could not make out from where I stood appeared on the porch of the house. Startled, I stopped, but Papa continued walking, his eyes now on the house. The echoing giggles of my lost sisters returned.

"Can we stop?" I cried out to him.

"Come!" he shouted.

He stopped in front of the house and it disappeared. Papa laughed. A small boy, naked except for a red baseball cap that floated over his head, turned to face us as his penis wagged below him. Papa continued laughing as the boy gripped a shiny golden rifle. He pointed the rifle our way and I attempted to pull my hand out of my father's grasp.

"Run!" I yelled, but he stayed still and concentrated on the young boy.

The boy lifted the weapon over his head and smirked. He then took the gun and, tilting his head back with an opened mouth, he slid it down his throat until it disappeared. When the boy was finished, he smacked his lips and vanished. Panting and crying now, I looked up at Papa, who appeared unmoved by what he had just seen. He stopped laughing and continued down the road, pulling my hand as I struggled to release myself.

Ahead of us several black dogs with drooping tongues barked viciously at us. Papa stopped walking and gazed at the large dogs.

"Run!" I screamed, and hid behind his back from the sight of the malevolent creatures.

"No. Come!" he shouted and took a step toward the dogs. They stopped barking, so he took another step. They then disappeared. When he took a third step toward where the dogs had challenged him, an army of rebels with guns and knives appeared in their place. Papa's eyes grew so wide that the bottom lids dropped to his chin.

"Run! They're coming!" I shouted. And still holding my hand, he turned around and ran in the opposite direction of the rebels. Dragged on my knees and bleeding as we ran, I looked back as the rebels gained speed and charged toward us.

"They're coming, Papa! They're coming!" I howled, and my father's laughter, along with the laughter of my lost sisters, pressed onto my ears.

"They're coming for us!" I belted and cried, attempting to gain footing to ease the blood from escaping my knees.

"Run. They're coming! They're coming for us! Run!" I shouted against the resonating cackles. I turned around again and a rebel's heartless face and eyes, his cruel lips and tongue, were in my face.

"They're coming!" I shouted again and he reached out his hand to grab my dress. I felt him gaining behind me and hollered.

When I opened my eyes, K ran away from the bed to stand with my Mam and Papa. The light glowered brightly above my head and my face and pillow were wet.

"Jesus," Mam said and raised a quavering hand to her mouth.

I was dreaming, I realized, and had somehow woken up everybody in the house with my screaming. I rubbed my eyes to see their faces clearly. They stood watching me. I sat up in bed and Mam and Papa finally came toward me with outstretched hands, careful as though I had been newly injured and they were afraid of breaking any more bones.

THIRTEEN

At those gatherings, weddings, funerals, where familiar names are stuttered through laughter, those who are old, while boasting of their meekness, will recall the steps that led them to Staten Island or Rhode Island or Minnesota or Atlanta or Maryland or Virginia or Tennessee. The conversation will bend and someone will always start a sentence with: "If the war had not happened . . ." and so on with the grandest plans, sweet to hear, hard to imagine. "If the war had not happened, Liberia would be a goliath in Africa by now" and "If the war had not happened, our lives would have been better" and "If the war had not happened my wife would have stayed" and they would have built their mansions in the mountains of Nimba, or Robertsport's beaches, among beds of palm trees, and I always laughed at this familiar song. There they shared the time when Rawlings closed his border at Togo and Liberia became a haven to the Ghanaians, and during Biafra, we were refuge to the Nigerians, and during the Korean War, how we helped the Koreans, and during World War II, how we helped the Americans. "If the war had not happened," they say. "If the coup had not happened," they say. Sweet to hear. Hard to imagine.

But there I was on that therapist's couch, in that small and dimly lit room, and within the words I said that night were:

"If the war had not happened."

I said: "If the war had not happened, we probably would have met in Liberia."

"Are you sure?"

"Maybe," I answered under my breath. "Our parents were very close friends. Still are. But before the war and everything. We met here, but we would have met there too. If everyone stayed."

She nodded and stared.

At some point in my teens I became intrigued with the number 8, and the number 62 was close to her angular brown face on psychologytoday .com, so I chose her. K mentioned I should consider being more thoughtful about my choice, but "at least I went" I told K after my first meeting. "It's weird. Talking to strangers about . . . my stuff. I don't think it's for me, but I'll give it a shot." A few months before, during my initial session on a cool Wednesday evening, I shared with the therapist my affinity for round numbers, and words, my appreciation of her lamp lighting, and, after some coercion, him. Her presence, her face, her voice were soft. I kept going back and eventually I did not mind having someone other than Mam or my sisters to pour into about things only they could know.

"What do you think the dream means?" the therapist asked after listening to ten minutes of my exact description of Satta and the details of that day.

"I don't know. The fact that she was holding the oil like a baby in all of the dreams she's shown up in is interesting. I've been thinking about going back," I said.

"Where?"

"To Liberia. I haven't been back since we left. No matter where we moved to, even when we were in Texas, I think I always knew I would go back."

"That makes sense. And how long were you in Texas again?" She leaned back and wrote on her notepad.

"Since I was eight. Eight to seventeen. Then I moved back here for school."

"I can imagine you're curious to see how it's changed. And to see your parents. It was a big change for them to move back after all these years. Brave."

"Yeah," I agreed.

"And you and your sisters and your younger brothers, you're all adults now, of course, but it sounds like that was still a big transition."

"It was. It is."

"You told me last week that *you* ended your recent relationship. Correct?" she asked softly, almost purring, and I welcomed it. "And since your breakup you've been having these night . . ."

"Dreams," I interrupted. "Yes."

"Right. You seem to still care for him. Do you ever consider going back?" she asked, her back straightened.

I must have been shaking my head, facing the window, or have rolled my eyes, taking too long to answer.

"Is that an upsetting question?" she asked.

"No, it's just . . . we weren't a good match. If it were easy of course I would go back, but I've been sad because I know it wouldn't be right, and he was like my family, so I lost a member of my family."

"I see."

"And the long distance. It's awful. It's not for me. I spend months at a time up there but how long could that go on for? There was no end in sight really. It made me feel like I was . . . running." She nodded again. "But honestly, I'm beginning to believe I've been discouraged for other reasons. Not the breakup."

"Yes, maybe. Leaving him was your choice," she insisted and it flustered me. "As I listen to you, I keep hearing themes of loss. When you experience it, as you've explained, the nightmares from your childhood, triggered by your past traumas, return . . ."

". . . I haven't been having nightmares."

"Well . . ."

"Just dreams. The woman, Satta. That's nothing like the dreams I had when I was a kid."

"Sure," she said, returning to her purr, "I understand. But they are strange enough that they've caused alarm."

"I didn't experience trauma in the way you're understanding it," I interrupted again.

"Oh?"

"This isn't one of those cases."

"One of what cases?" she asked before we fell into a silence.

"I believe I had a happy childhood. That's my point. I don't think of trauma in that way. I don't want to sound ungrateful or spoiled."

"Recognizing pain is not ungrateful," she said.

"Nothing horrible happened to me. At least I don't think it did. I think I was lucky," I managed to say without crying, although the tears lurked, menaced.

"Your family was tremendously fortunate to have made it out unharmed," she said nodding.

"Mostly. My grandfather . . ."

"What happened to your grandfather?" Sixty-Two asked and waited.

"Rebels," I forced out. "He left the village to get us food and medicine, and rebels killed him. They thought he was a Mandingo man. My mother's family is Vai. He was very tall, and a Muslim, and he wore a kufi, so they thought he was Mandingo. And the Mandingo tribe sided with the Krahn people during the war, and even before, and the Krahn people were . . ."

"The president's people, right?"

"Yeah. Samuel Doe's people."

There were few instances when I remembered saying his name out loud. It wasn't until my twenties that I finally brought myself to watch the beginning of Doe's taped assassination. I stared at my computer screen and recalled my childhood fantasies, the oblivion, the surprise I still felt in knowing this man, who for so long I imagined as a fire-breathing dragon, had a face, glasses, a human body, human tears.

"And the Mandingo and Krahn people, mostly government soldiers, were killing Gio and Mano people because of an old conflict when one of them almost overtook Doe's administration. And there were other minor conflicts, of course, other motivations," I said, trailing off the familiar recitation, something I'd memorized in high school to explain what had happened in my childhood country, to explain myself.

"But. My father and my grandmother worked overtime to protect us from trauma. The kind of trauma that would stem from that kind of carnage, you know?"

I watched her eyes carefully to see if she understood. If she was seeing me, or if my revelations fit me neatly into a box labeled trauma.

"I feel guilty maybe. Ungrateful, that I became so sad after the breakup. Because I think I was lucky. My father protected us from understanding what it was that was going on. The intensity of it all."

"I see," she said. And then there was that familiar silence. "Yet you understood, you mentioned. You did know."

"Kind of," I murmured. "Eventually. Yes."

She wrote something down. She waited for me to continue.

"I think, as women of color, especially women of color who come from some means, any means really, we tend to play down the unpleasant things we've experienced. To bury them," she said finally.

"Maybe," I responded.

"Perfection or the desire for it, it becomes a mask . . . a uniform. But there is something underneath. What's underneath makes us real."

I thought of Mam in that moment. She had taught me many things, and at times, especially during those teenage years of promising her I would move far away to New York as soon as I got my diploma, she was more than I deserved. She taught me how to cook, how to write, my posture, how to care for a home, how to love God, how to read. She taught me politeness, creativity, how to write a letter, especially to those who had offended me. How to pray, how to fold clothes, how to love my sisters, how to love my brothers, how to love myself. She taught me about women—how to be one, how to know them, how to befriend them, how to give advice and love them, and how some would betray me because they saw kindness as weakness, and at the first sign of such brutality I should walk away, for such women did not even love themselves. That not all who chose to be around me liked me. That some knew too well how to pretend, and they would raise daughters with these doctrines, so I should remember her words and the words of my Ol' Mas to raise mine. And some would raise sons they did not want to let go of, and would handle them like marionettes, and I should be careful never to sit in the audience of such a show for too long.

But there were things I went into the world not knowing. We did not talk about what to do when a boy was unkind, in words or actions, breaking my heart. I was lousy in the ways of healing. Mam had one true love and she married him. She had one true love in a country of women like her, whose sun took turns resting on their deep, dark skin. My true loves in our new country, by either inheritance or indoctrination, were taught that black women were the least among them. Loving me was an act of resistance, though many did not know it. And Mam could not understand this feeling, the heaviness of it, to be loved as resistance, as an exception to a rule. To fight to be seen in love, to stay in love throughout the resistance. This was my new country.

In middle school most of the faces around me were white. There was one black boy I thought I would marry, before I knew the meaning. He wrote me a letter, folded at both ends. He told me I was beautiful, but that my skin was too dark and he couldn't date a dark-skinned woman. In high school after I became homecoming queen, after being crowned under those Friday-night lights, a single black feminine body in the middle of that green turf, overlooking a sea of American dreaming, that same boy came up to me at the edge of the field and whispered, "I told you that you were beautiful." And if my childhood dragons wanted me to believe that I had no home, no country, no place in this world, the monsters in my new home, in that statement, consented, complied: I could be beautiful in a place and still not enough, not because of who I was or anything I had done, but because of something as simple, and somehow as grand in this new place, as the color of my skin.

In college I dated black men who previously only dated white women, although they were certain they did not have a type. In my twenties, in Harlem, I occasionally found myself in the arms of men who admitted I was the first dark-skinned woman they had ever been in a serious relationship with—the others were black women who were light, fair, racially ambiguous. "But you're better looking than all of my exes, to be honest. Even being dark-skinned," they would say, as if giving me a compliment. In my thirties, a man I loved told me I was beautiful in the same breath that he admitted he did not believe I was physically enchanting enough for mainstream American audiences, the first to throw a stone at my dreams of Hollywood. Mam did not know the ways of this—the indoctrination of a black woman socialized here. I found I loved her more for that. That she never told me to stay out of the sun when it was highest. Never obsessed over my edges being straight enough that maybe the boys would forget my blackness when they looked at my hair. I enjoyed the sun like any child should, while many of my friends hid in the shade. Mam never feared her blackness. So I never feared my blackness, until the men.

How does it feel to be an exception? They taught me. Then they led me to that conversation. To the purring woman casually mentioning my traumas. Love gives us the coordinates to these rooms.

I may have shrugged.

"What you and your family have been able to do in this country . . . it's something. But that doesn't erase those months during your childhood, and the attention it all deserves."

"Honestly, I had an experience in Texas that was more traumatic than the war," I said quickly, casually.

"And still . . . that still does not erase the war's trauma," she insisted.

"Sure, sure. I understand what you mean. But what I'm saying is, they protected us. They did whatever they could to protect us. I had a happy childhood. A blessed childhood."

"They seem like wonderful people. And your mother," she added, and I could tell she was closely watching my face. "But that doesn't mean what you experienced was any less harmful. The childhood nightmares, your recurring dreams, they seem to be triggered when you experience feelings of loss . . . which makes sense. That's a chapter of life it sounds like you never confronted. And your feelings of loss, your ability to deal with the adjustment to your new life after that trauma, even to your relationships, that's all connected. And I wonder if . . . if you've thought of your recent relationships in that way."

"In what way?"

"Well . . . what makes *you* leave?" she asked.

"A number of things have made me leave. But . . . I don't think it's linked to anything from my childhood."

She gave me a Mam look. One that believed that everything is linked to everything else. What we have done to what we are doing, from where we've come to where we're going, our five-year-old actions to this morning's breakfast.

"Texas," she began again. "Tell me about your time there."

In the seventh grade, we were allowed to sit where we wanted in the lunchroom, and on my first day of this freedom, I sat with them. It was not a conscious choice, it was more a forced understanding that the table was the only place we belonged; so every day my gangly legs reached our haven in the back of the lunchroom where there was an empty seat waiting for me to sit with a dozen or so Blackgirls among the hundreds of white faces of our suburban middle school.

I had become inconspicuous, not only sounding and dressing like my classmates, but acting like them as well. At the table, I was still African, but I was one of them. Every day at lunch I went to our table, an array of brown faces with glossed lips, and either braids or shoulder-length relaxed hair. We were friends but we barely had anything in common. Except that we were black. Some of us athletes. Two of us in honors classes. Different interests, different backgrounds, different styles, different hygiene, different daddy stories, different momma stories, different tastes in boys, different accents, different grades, different, but we were friends because we were all black.

If we were beautiful then, we did not know it. True confidence was much too tiresome a pursuit, so we pretended. We were barely on television except for that channel, in the books we read except for that chapter, or in the magazines, and damn those magazines. They did not see us except when we were together. They called us the Blackgirl table and we did not mind it because they thought we were cool. And to maintain this blackness, this shiny, special thing that was bigger than any other part of our identity, so big that it had to go first—in order to maintain this blackness, we mimicked the only representations we saw of ourselves on those channels and in those books and in those magazines. We spoke louder, shouted even, yelled at each other in jest when we entered rooms. We created a language of gestures bigger than ourselves. We were children and how else would they see us? We performed our race, our prefix. When the others wanted to be our friends, they came to us snapping their fingers—though they were usually well-meaning people and could not know they were offensive—sometimes even rolling their eyes and placing nervous fists upon their waists.

These others, they didn't ask us, when we were all together, about papers or school. Never about school. Never math or how well we did on the last test. That was not our purpose. We were the Blackgirls. Not Jasmin, not Kim, not Shabreka, not Olu, not Martina, not Charlotte, not Ashley, not Christine, not Jareika, not Sheri, not Roxanne, not Emily, not Ebony, not Lauren, not Sara, not Whitney, not Sheika, not me.

By then my experiences in my kindergarten class in Monrovia were a distant memory, the ease, the orange tint of mornings, the not knowing that the color of my skin they considered a stain across the ocean.

Spring, Texas, was a working- and middle-class suburbia that bordered one or two horse ranches and a shooting range. The residents were mostly peaceful, well meaning, and conservative. My parents quickly found a church they liked and we spent three days a week wedged between the pews, singing Southern Baptist hymns from memory. Because it was a white church, for us as we were growing up, Brother so-and-so and Sister so-and-so were all white. For Mam and Papa, Christ was their race and Christians, all Christians, were treated like extended family. They looked for God in people before they looked to skin color for clues on how the relationship would unfold. Casually watching basketball games, Papa would sometimes say, unprompted, "You know that guy is a believer" with pride, as if he knew him personally. I noticed this difference when I went to friends' houses, where the phrase "you know how white folks are" first entered my psyche and made some things that happened in our new country make sense.

The children I attended middle school with were the same who stared at me on the first day I entered the citrus-smelling elementary school after our move to Texas. They knew my name and found it "neat" that I was African, all smiling, all curious, especially when they saw Mam at school events wearing a traditional lappa rather than one of the many pairs of jeans she had recently purchased. I did not talk about the war or Liberia beyond my classmates' general knowledge that I was "African." I did not have the time to give while I was trying to understand that in this new place that Mam and Papa had told us was home, skin color was king—king above nationality, king above life stories, and, yes, even king above Christ.

In one of the houses we rented in Spring, the corner store was at the end of our street, a little over two hundred yards away from our house. I walked there one day with the Blackgirls. Mam was home making us dinner after track practice and I remember she told us we should just stay and wait for the food, but the Blackgirls and I wanted to follow my big sister and her friends. It was track season, it was early spring. The corner store had only about five aisles of goods and a wall cooler that held beer and soft drinks. It was an old store at the corner of a strip mall that included a billiards club, a hardware store, and a day care center. The shelves were organized in a way that put a pack of sunflower seeds right beside a generic brand of deodorant and below eight different assortments of prophylactics. When we entered, one of the Blackgirls was being playfully teased by one of my sister's friends, whom we met at the store. We were being loud. The cashiers looked at each one of our faces as we passed.

"Hello," I said.

There were two men behind the counter. They looked similar to one another but one was noticeably older with thick glasses and a bright red face. Neither of them spoke. We roamed the aisles and stopped in front of the candy, where we took our pick of Airheads, Now and Laters, bubble gum, Starbursts, and chocolate bars. I could not decide between Skittles and a Hershey's bar, so while the others headed to the freezer for their drinks, I stayed in the aisle and stared down at the candy. In my peripheral vision I saw the younger cashier look at me from the end of the aisle. I looked at him and smiled. He nodded toward me and looked past me at my sister and friends. When they finished getting their drinks, they walked to the front of the store and crowded the cashier. The older man began to ring up their things, and I stayed in the aisle looking at the Skittles bag and brown candy bar.

"Which one will you have?" I heard a long drawl at the end of the aisle. I expected that he was still there—after all, we had all been watched at stores before. But it was the first time that someone had spoken to me after watching me as intently as he had. I looked down to make sure that the candy was still in my hands, that I had not mistakenly opened it while daydreaming. The red and brown pack rested in my palms, yet I knew shortly after the man spoke that something was about to go desperately wrong.

"Everything okay?" my sister asked.

"Yeah," I said and placed the Skittles back on the shelf. We headed to the cashier, where the other girls waited for us. By then the Blackgirls were fidgeting and noticeably disturbed by the store owner's demeanor.

"Sorry I took so long," I said. I placed my candy bar on the counter and waited for the older man to ring it up. It was eighty-four cents and I reached into my pocket for three quarters and a dime. I placed the three quarters on the counter and reached for the dime but I could not find it. I checked the other pocket but it was not there.

"What do you need?" my sister asked.

"Nine cents. I thought I had a dime," I said.

At once the Blackgirls reached into their pockets to help me pay my deficit.

"Ridiculous," the cashier murmured as we searched. He said curse words, and we huddled together, as if the warmth of our bodies would protect us, steady us in that moment. Wi slammed a quarter onto the counter, making us all jump.

"What's ridiculous?" she asked.

"Ol' racist man. Just give us our change so we can go!" my sister's friend added.

We were all taken aback by her accusation, though we thought the same. We were all afraid. Not as brave as her. "Racist? Who's racist?" the younger man said from behind. We turned around.

"You've been watching us since we walked in," her friend said, stepping toward him.

"That's it, then!" the cashier said, throwing the change from my purchase onto the counter, so hard that some pennies were flung onto the floor and landed at our feet. "Get on out of here then! Get out before I call the cops! We don't want trouble—just get out!"

The man's face turned more crimson as he shouted. We did not bother picking up the coins. We headed out of the store, embarrassed and humiliated, and Wi stayed behind with her friends in a full-out screaming match with the two owners. I wanted to go home and get Mam. As soon as I closed the door, I heard a loud crash inside the store. I turned around quickly and saw Wi run toward me with tussled hair and tears covering her face.

"Come on!" she yelled, pulling my hand. The younger store owner chased them out of the store waving a broomstick. Run.

"Get out of here!" he yelled as he stomped the concrete on the road back to our house.

"You niggers! Get on out of here!" he yelled, though his voice was now faint as it hit the back of our heads. Sobs flew beside me—the running cries of my sister and her friends. The dragons had different mothers here, and we ran. We ran. Again. Niggers, he shouted. An animal, a brute, an ignorant person, an unrighteous person. But we were little girls. Niggers, from a man who probably did not see color. But how could he see color? He did not see us.

His voice faded to a moan. And as we sprinted and the memory of the word flew past us and our heads swayed against the wind, I wanted only to see Mam—to hear that he was wrong, to press my face into her core until the sound of the world wholly stopped, to have her explain this new country to me in a way she never could. Wanted to see beyond the tears but they kept coming down. Wanted to return to the grim fantasies of my daydreams but I could not find them. Could not hear more than my sisters crying. Could not see my home though it was so close. Could not see my Mam though I knew she was there. Legs and stomach hurt from sprinting. Thoughts a blunder and I was finally awake.

ASIDE:

WHEN THE THERAPIST SUGGESTS
I BEGIN DATING AGAIN

FOURTEEN

Leo. He's a photographer. BU. He's five feet ten. Three pictures all of himself against walls (one brick wall, outside, side profile) holding his camera. One of his hands on his dog. A hound. The dog looks disappointed in him. A picture in Johannesburg or Port-au-Prince or some other Black country where he's surrounded by a dozen five-year-olds in uniform, just as ashy and carefree as you were at that age, holding up peace signs. He's smiling with his mouth open.
Left.

Oran. He's a photographer. NYU. He's six feet. There's a picture of him taking a picture. Another in a suit with a press pass, against a *Hamptons* magazine step-and-repeat. Another on an air mattress with a tiger. His camera is in one hand, a baby's bottle in the other.
Left.

Vick. He's a photographer. SVA. He has no height. Nothing expository. He takes pictures with celebrities, and he isn't smiling in any of them. Not even in the one with Jason Statham. He's kind of cute, but
Left.

Sammy. Sammy has no height or education. Sammy has no profession. Sammy has one blurry photograph of the right side of his face. He's looking out of a window squinting. Sammy doesn't want to play games. Sammy is looking for the real deal. Sammy knows people get on here to get laid. Sammy doesn't want that. He wants to wash your hair. He wants to make love to your mind. He's sick of vain women, sick of New York. Sammy is a lover. The only lover
Left.

Ivan. Ivan is six feet. Brooklyn College. Ivan has muscles. Ivan likes to party. All of Ivan's pictures are taken with friends at clubs. Oh, wait, Ivan has one photo alone. Ivan and his muscles and some Oakleys are on a yacht with an opened beer bottle and Ivan left his last fuck on shore. Ivan wants you to know that looks can be deceiving. He's a teddy bear, he says. Swipe right and
Left.

Neil. He's five feet eight. Pretty face. Morehouse man. Very straight teeth. Very white teeth. He's been through some thangs and he wants you to know. He's over his savage ways. He's grown now and wants a grown-ass woman to hold him down. Neil is also the real deal. He wants a girl who will be with him through the good and the bad. He wants a lifetime partner. He knows this is just an app.
Left.

Etienne. Etienne is wearing Freddy Krueger gloves in a bathroom mirror.
Left.

Tremaine. Hates bitches who swipe left and don't respond to him. He hates games. Tremaine is looking for a real one. He's ready for his Halle Berry though he looks like a seductive moose.
Left.

Ibn. Oh no, I know Ibn.
LEFT.

Mason. He's fine, y'all. We have some mutual friends. Mason went to Yale. Mason is five feet eleven. Mason likes Murakami books and Vice News. Mason likes Ta-Nehisi Coates. Mason mentors kids, y'all. He watches Bill Maher. Mason is new to this thing, this online dating thing. Mason is a lawyer. Mason is an MD/MBA. He has very white teeth. He winked at the camera after Tough Mudder. Mason likes button-ups and attended the Veuve Clicquot Polo Classic last year. Mason has style.
Left.

Ian. He's six feet. NYU. Not much information, but he's Christian and he quotes Scripture and he's wearing a Commes des Garçons sweater. He's cute, he works in finance, which, ugh, but whatever. He has a nice smile. He lives a mile and six-tenths miles away so no long distance. No bathroom selfies, no tigers. Whatever.   Right.
    ian messages right away. ian wants you to sit on his face.

three-month interlude
during which time you learn the man you almost married has found someone else. they're casually dating, a mutual friend tells you while looking at the ceiling, as if describing the contents of a soju cocktail. you want to shake her. this is your *life*. how? it's been about seven months, she says. but the last you heard he was broken too. you're dating, too, she reminds you and good because we won't be in our twenties for long and so what? you've been seeing a therapist and the last you heard he had been writing you a letter and he worked on it every day and he wanted to make sure it was perfect before sending it. the last you heard he was at a party and he was sober. and he was hiding, how the *hell*? and where? where did she find him hiding?

Tailor. Tailor is six feet. Tailor is in real estate. Tailor lists no school. Tailor likes to read, he likes films, he likes Brooklyn.
                Right.

FIFTEEN

Deda texted. I did not immediately answer. It said: "Did you read the article I sent?" I was on my way to meet a boy and I was late again. I had canceled an appointment with the therapist, my second in a row. I changed my clothes more times than I could count and I almost sent a picture of the unremarkable dress to Wi for the boost I so desperately needed, the kind only she could give, with intentional spelling errors only teachers would make, and too many emojis. In high school we did not have cell phones. No picture messages. Back then we got ready at each other's houses with Brandy and Destiny's Child blasting in the background. That night, I did not send the picture.

I should not have read the article before the date but I did. In the subway on my way to meet that boy. The article was another one of those institute memos, those think pieces, those essays based on empirical data of the select pool variety. Apparently assortive mating is less and less an option for black women. Our eyelashes not curled at the right angle. We're prescriptive, wrongly named, we are undesirable again. We are the most likely to be swiped left, they say. We are drowning in our degrees and our solo travels and each other again. Who wrote this?

I met up with him at a dive bar and I hoped he would remember my face before I would have to recall his. I promised this friend a few weeks before that I would stop ignoring men in the street after she sent me an essay about old-fashioned meetings—those "in church" "supermarket" "bumped into each other in the street" impossibilities that were once our religion. So I met this boy, this Johnny Boy, in the street. I never would have done that in my twenties but I have grown. I know better now than not to live. Two weeks later I was at a dive bar, nose in my phone, being corrupted by the contemporary doctrines of my unlovability and the reasons for it.

"Hey," he said, almost shouting, almost afraid to touch my shoulder. We found a seat in a corner underneath a John Wayne poster, lit from above with a few strings of old Christmas lights, dingy lights of pastel colors that blinked to the rhythm of those songs I had not heard in some time.

"What were you reading?" Johnny Boy asked as if he had known me for years, as if this was not his first time asking me that question. Familiar. Is this how love stories in a woman's thirties begin? I would not mind.

"Oh just . . . some essay," I answered and blushed. And I guess I was too eager to hide my phone, because he prodded. "It's about . . . it's some essay about how difficult it is for black women to find husbands," I said finally, I think laughing, just as the waitress approached our table, and she feigned a smile, an awkward smile, and glanced at him before rushing through our drink orders. She had heard me. When she left, Johnny Boy was smiling, a nervous smile, but confident. He knew he was handsome. He said: "Those things can be annoying." My eyes questioned. "How everything is about race now, you know?" he continued, still nervous but unflinching. Neither of us knew what it meant. I felt guilty for finding his ignorance endearing. "I mean, I've dated black girls before and it's been all good. I know other people who date . . . you know . . . I just . . . I don't see color."

Nika emailed. "Did you read that piece about the rise of black girl/white boy relationships?" she sent with the link. I was swirling. That's what they called it. Johnny Boy was different. Johnny Boy from the

Midwest, from the West Coast, from New Jersey. He grew on me but people looked at us as we walked hand in hand, as though we were naked, but deformed, and they did not know if they should be offended or feel sorry for us—us, those contrasting colors interlocked. Brooklyn was finicky in that way. It boasts of its progressiveness while at the same time is surprised by it, like an objectively beautiful yet insecure woman. I showed Johnny Boy the article that night and he laughed, as I thought he would. Then he said: You and your friends talk about race a lot. We do? I asked. And he nodded, a concerned nod, one with weight, one asking. Race was everywhere here, the here I called home now, although Johnny Boy avoided those conversations, although he could not see it. So instead we laughed as much as we could, visited botanical gardens while he compared me to flowers, listened to records, went dancing, ate with friends, spoke to Mam and Papa on speaker, took a road trip, grocery shopped, went to the dog park, went shopping for pants for his interview, went shopping for a dress for that date night, went to a Liberian restaurant he had found online in Queens, because he thought I would like it, went to the movies, went to shows, went to the Bronx, went to my accountant one time, but never went there. And progress kept looking, kept staring, kept wondering what it was about him, or about me, that made us flaunt our corruption in that way.

He was left. Far left. It was 2013 or 2014 and he was white and the Blackgirls were dying and the Blackboys were dying. He was angry. He felt guilty and ashamed. He was ambivalent. He touched my face. He kissed me long. He hated what happened to those countries in Africa. What happened to my family—our having to run and hide. He hated what was happening to those cities in the Midwest. Listened when I told him I'd experienced a thing again, at a store or at the office or on the street, and I thought the thing had happened because of my skin. It was because I was black in this kingdom where black was criminal, a stain, a deformity. A thing had happened and it reminded me of the first time—that time when I was a kid and I took too long to get my candy bar and that store owner pushed my sister and called us that word. But that was Texas, he said. But this is New York, he said. It doesn't matter, it's everywhere in this country, I said. I'm sorry, he said. I don't understand some people. We are all the same, he said. Our world would be so much stronger if we stopped seeing color.

So he marched with me. He squeezed my hand throughout Brooklyn. But the weight of those girls and boys dying was heavy on my shoulders, their names made a home on my tongue. I wondered who they were, how many things had happened before the one that finally took their lives. And Johnny Boy and I drifted apart because the heavier the burden on my shoulders, the harder I typed into the night, the more New York began to look like Texas began to look like California began to look like Baltimore began to look like Florida. The more Johnny Boy reminded me of his blindness to the thing, of his love for me through the thing. Why didn't he see me? There were times he held my hand through the night. Those contrasting colors interlocked. Gray eyes in the moonlight. You are special, he said, and I love you, he said, let me love you. And I never said it back. I needed time, I said, I'm just getting over my last relationship. Why do we make the ones who love us wait?

Ashleigh called. She was crying. She wanted to hear my voice. I missed her though I had seen her a week before. My phone was cold and still I pressed it to my ear when I heard her whimper. We were in the news. We were trending again. George Zimmerman was still free. Eric Garner had been choked to death. Michael Brown was an unarmed black boy who was shot six times, at least two in the head, and it had killed him. I know, girl, I eased her. We'll march and call the congressmen, I said. Write a think piece, I said. Write letters, I said, in this our country. But she told me in these moments she felt worthless. Each one made her feel worthless. Invisible again. Depressed again. Her tears sounded familiar. Like that day in middle school running with the Blackgirls, that cutting music that would replay for the rest of our lives. My friends, these women I hid with during storms, these women I consumed so many of those joyous Brooklyn hours with. And I want to find the words, the poetry, to give her the thanks she deserves for her shoulder. For stirring my ginger tea all those times my voice got lost in that job/man/city. For understanding what it was like to be at that table, to be a young girl just learning how much the world's opinion of you differed from your loving Mam's. Those girls helped me. They healed me. She heals me. But another thing had happened and she forgot her power. Another thing happens and she becomes that little girl, running. Racing to safety, to be better than each other, to be better than ourselves, to be seen.

In the shower that night I thought of our conversation, her tears. I had taken my braids out because I wanted to run my fingers through my roots, my coils, to be reminded. I heard the front door open from inside the bathroom, and Johnny Boy shouted hello and what are you doing? I am washing my hair, I yelled back. I took my braids out. Oh, your 'fro is out. Your 'fro is out again, he joked. Doesn't washing it take forever, he asked, and I could tell he was smiling. I didn't answer him. Well, I guess we won't be going out to dinner tonight, he said. Don't you wish you had hair like mine? he asked. I felt a chill. Of rage, shock, perplexity, exhaustion, something. I was not finished but I turned off the faucet right away. Right away. Foam slid off my body and beads of water from my natural curls fell to my shoulders. I heard my breathing in my ears. WHAT THE FUCK DID YOU JUST SAY? I asked. And in the aftermath of the questions, in the silence, he could still hear my anger in my breathing, and I heard his footsteps approach the room. Wait, whoa, what? What did I? No, it was a joke. I'm sorry. It was a bad, bad joke, babe. Babe. I'm sorry. I'm so sorry. And he rambled and was still rambling when I opened the door, naked but not deformed, and the water was coming from my hair, but then the water was coming from my eyes. He had done a thing. But I would not run from him. He stared at me, dared not touch me, sorry, and I knew it. But he had said a thing and that day had already broken me. And I could still hear that cutting music. So loud, it echoed, so I stood there until we both knew. Stood there until the echoes finished.

Springtime. Johnny Boy had been kind, he was good, and I lacked patience. Men like him were the men I grew up with. All-American and well meaning, painstakingly oblivious of their privilege. Most days with him reminded me of the life I traded for New York. What would have become of the day we finally moved into that house if I had closed my eyes and stayed?

On the day my family moved into our first house in America, the sun, although invisible behind the motionless clouds, had already risen onto the cul-de-sac. Knowing somehow that it was there, though she could not see it nor did she ever see it at the time she rose every morning, Mam was already awake and packing old silverware that she refused to discard and newly purchased china sets into a cupboard that she had picked out only months before. After she unpacked each box, she balled her freckled hands into a fist and released her slightly wrinkled fingers into the air. In Liberia when Papa built their first house in Caldwell, she did not reap the enjoyment of unpacking because there were always hands around waiting to meet her needs or requests as they came. And she always said that just when she began to fall for it, she left for New York. There were days she spoke of Caldwell, which she said she imagined was muddied with broken sticks of wood that formed nothing more than the shapes of Liberia's recent chapter, that hosted nothing more than companies of squatters and their poorly strewn tents and many children.

So she and Wi had planted a palm tree outside of that Texan home, similar to one of her trees in Caldwell. And looking at the tree that day, ripe baby leaves lifting slowly in and out of sleep from the morning breeze, the voices of new neighbors clamoring around us since the cunning narrative of Y2K had finally died down, and subsequently everyone resumed buying houses in suburban cul-de-sacs and carried on waiting for Godot, I knew I wanted to leave. I could not believe the new walls and hallway. I could not believe the arched doors and frames, the clear glass windows that overlooked our new street in the home that was now our own. Not borrowed, not rented, but ours, ten years after moving to our new country. I heard them all laughing downstairs. Yet. There was that restlessness again, and then, the understanding that the quiet life outside our front door, beyond that driveway, did not match my internal melody. It never had.

I had learned Vai when I was five years old and forgotten it by the time I was six. At eight I traded fufu and soup for McDonald's Happy Meals, although the starch had been my favorite thing to eat for years and one of my first words. At thirteen I folded the lappa suits my Ol' Ma and aunties mailed from Logan Town and ELWA, 10 Monrovia 100 Liberia, in favor of Express and NY & Co. jeans, although they never correctly fit my too-skinny waist and hips.

Mam noticed our new interests when we were teenagers, and dishes like cassava leaf and palaver sauce took a back seat to spaghetti and meatloaf when we had friends visiting. During the week, when friends and teammates from Little League, dance squads, and basketball teams raided her house, she would come downstairs and speak, spend time listening to our stories or the laughter shared after games, and then she would go upstairs and rest.

"You don't mind, do you?" we asked her as we turned down the penetrating drums and cymbals of Nimba Burr, Miatta Fahnbulleh, Fela and Femi Kuti for musical alternatives that our friends could recognize.

"No, I don't mind," she would say, smiling without teeth.

We were at my high school on an open house night. Mam wore a lappa suit with colors that nearly parted the sea of white faces in the hallway as we walked. We arrived in class and the teacher greeted me and Mam. We found two empty seats. I saw familiar faces of classmates. Most of them resembled their mothers and fathers; some of them came with grandparents. I smiled at class friends when they caught my eye. They grinned back, then surveyed Mam's lappa suit in bewilderment. My legs shook nervously throughout. I saw them look at her as though she was from another planet, a species they had only briefly skimmed in history books and at museums. They all seemed alike. Khaki Dickies or dress slacks; button-up blouses or T-shirts with the face of our school mascot plastered across their breasts; stringy blond hair pulled back in a ponytail or worn down their shoulders with feathered bangs just above their eyelids; blue and green and brown eyes all passing by the corner where my mother and I sat; pink and red lips; white and yellow teeth; pale and tan hands; fat and skinny necks. And there was our beautiful Mam—a legend, a relic, an enigma. Toward the end of the teacher's presentation, Mam raised her hand and asked a question. She had to repeat herself, but she was gracious, always gracious, and I, I was silent during the entire drive home.

"What's wrong?" she asked as she parked in our driveway.

"Nothing," I answered and turned toward the door to exit the car.

"You haven't said anything. What's wrong?"

The moonlight bounced off her cheeks and her breath grew rapid in the silence.

I said nothing, but then I said something stupid, like she could have asked me rather than having to repeat herself, because some people didn't understand her accent. She was taken aback because she was a teacher, a successful teacher recognized by the state, and she spoke all day, and she said her students had no issues with her accent. I said it wasn't a big deal.

"It is a big deal. You brought it up," Mam said.

"Well, maybe next time just ask me afterward. I hate those things anyway and didn't want to stay longer than we had to. Nobody did," I said.

"They make you not want your mother to sound African in school now, then? That's what we sending you to school for?"

"No—"

"I am African. And so are you!" Mam's voice cracked as the locusts cried outside our car, along the narrow driveway that led to our new house, a house that never quite blended with the rest.

"Look at me," she said. "Are you ashamed of me?"

"No," I must have said.

"Good," she continued. "Because if you're ashamed of me, then you're ashamed of yourself."

I wanted to argue with her but I had neither the energy nor the courage to lie to her that I had not been proselytized, that I was not a victim of an education that did not have her in mind.

"You are African," she said, tears streaming. "The book, the book they show you with Africans in jungles with no clothes. You know better. Don't let them make you shame, yeh? You are African." The words hurt more than I had imagined. I had never heard them until that night. You are African. You are African. You are African: together so profoundly accusatory and judgmental that I wanted to run out of the car screaming. You are African, and it made me want to clench my fists and fight. And I did not know why.

"You hear me?" Mam stepped out of the car and slammed the door. I watched her lappa suit disappear into the house before I opened my door to the night's chorus.

When I entered the house, Mam was still in the foyer, frozen in front of the television that blared throughout the living room. Papa was leaned forward on the couch, carefully minding a BBC report on Liberia.

"They may start fighting again-oh," Papa said, shaking his head.

A reporter spoke over a camera shot of civilians running from crossfire with small bags of belongings and children on their backs and waists. They looked like Papa and Mam. They looked like my sisters and brothers, like me. According to the reporter, people had begun to evacuate after a bomb went off in Monrovia, but ECOWAS—a regional union of African states—and the United Nations had recently stepped in to negotiate with Charles Taylor and his rebel opposition. The civilians ran quickly as pieces of their belongings fell on the road behind them.

"They may start fighting again," Papa repeated himself, hypnotized by the images on the screen. "Ay-yah!" Mam said as the tears from outside dried on her cheeks and new ones took their place. Mam's shoulders shook and she surrendered to her sadness. When Papa noticed that she was crying, he stood straight and put his arm around her. He looked over Mam's dropped head at my face for answers.

I shrugged and went to my room. And that night I had another nightmare. I woke up, nearly a woman now underneath my thin nightgown, and I pulled open the door to my parents' room where a thin stream of light ran across their bodies. I wanted to sleep between them, as I had done as a child, but Mam felt so far from me—my denial of her now a disheveled bridge across a wayward stream of our misunderstanding. I lay at the foot of their bed, and it did not take long for Mam to rise and grab me a pillow and throw, find her way to me, and hug me back to sleep.

SIXTEEN

"Guess what!" my friend Tina yelped as soon as I hugged her hello. I welcomed her excitement after the monotony of blank screens and wasted time in front of that novel, and the writer's anxiety it caused. We met at a local museum and I knew as she approached, by how quickly she walked toward me with the anxiousness of those who are running away from one thing while running toward another, that there was news.

"What?" I asked, entering the building.

"I found out my ancestors are from Ghana." I smiled as she sang the country's name.

"That's cool, girl. DNA tests are great."

"Oh my God, I've been there before but I'm going back with my cousin by the end of the year."

"That's dope," I said, still smiling, and we proceeded through the exhibit while I brought up another topic of discussion, which Tina freely indulged.

That night she called me, energetically low, unpredictably upset.

I was, as Tina explained, not as supportive as she had imagined I would be. As an African-American whose history and heritage had been stolen during the transatlantic slave trade, she reminded me that her family had no place on the continent to call home in the way that mine had, and she expected that I would be happier for her.

"I was happy for you. I *am* happy for you," I insisted. "What was I supposed to do? Jump up and down?"

She said nothing, so I knew the answer was, perhaps, yes.

"I'm sorry," I said when the silence made a home. "I'm so sorry." For not being as supportive as she needed. For that history and those ships, I am so sorry.

"I guess I don't know what I was expecting," she said. But I knew. I understood.

She was not the first friend I had who had tested their blood for traces of a stolen home. I would often get calls about either DNA results or news that they were dating an African, usually a Nigerian guy who had just become comfortable with his foreign identity after years of being teased in grade school. Being from Africa was now cool and those boys knew it. My cousins, my friends, the boys I met in college who hid their too-long middle names with ritual emulation of their American friends, overusing "nigga" to camouflage the smell of okra sauce and fried fish, now changed their profile icons to West African flags and I wondered: What took us so long?

"I mean, I guess you're pretty Americanized anyway, so I get it," Tina said. "You don't talk about Liberia *that* much."

And where could I begin to tell that story? I ignored the comment because the admission would feel like rocks in my mouth—that Liberia lived with me every night, in my dreams, that I wear it on my skin and in the rhythm of my love stories. Where could I begin to tell her that there were dragons there too? That going to Ghana could give her a kind of peace, yes, but not the kind she was looking for. To say that would be to break her heart and I could not. She did not want or need the truth of her homegoing—not the whole truth. Tina wanted Kwame Nkrumah's Africa and William Tolbert's Africa and Thomas Sankara's Africa and Félix Houphouët-Boigny's. And we dream perhaps one day their versions of Ghana and Liberia and Burkina Faso and Ivory Coast will be resurrected. But those of us who have been pushed into new homes, new countries, know that our dragons killed those places too.

After Johnny Boy, there was the dream again of Satta and the jug of palm oil and when I woke up, every time I woke up, I felt like I was floating, like I was being carried, but to where?

Johnny Boy would say, "You're black, but not in the same way." As if it was both an indictment and a compliment, and it always made me look down, mostly in guilt, because he said it as more of a compliment than an indictment. A friend once told me that this was the same for the Blackgirls who were asked if they were mixed, or praised for their thin noses or their eye color—but what was so wrong with being black "in the same way"? "You're African, not really like American black. So why do you take all of this race stuff so seriously?" he asked.

That man at the store that day, the one who said that thing, he did not see African girls or Creole girls or girls who could trace their lines to Carolina plantations. He saw us, all of us, as Blackgirls. As the same. "Most people process the world not as they are, but as they are treated," I said to Johnny Boy. What I did not admit was even at that table and the years after, even after adopting the rage of my new sisters, I sometimes felt like an impostor. And similarly, my breathing would never temper at those family reunions and Monrovian elsewheres, hearing those stories of Liberia older than my years, than my memory.

So we—transplanted from Liberia and Nigeria and Ethiopia, from Ghana and Senegal and the DRC, from Kenya, from Zambia and elsewhere, pushed over the ocean by those scales and gnashing teeth, some before our parents and some after, some undocumented and some the first in their families born with blue passports—we practice what it is like to be black, to be white, to be American, to be anything other than who we are. Learn the words, the customs, the rage, the ways that our parents have not been here long enough to pass down. We took the teasing, the name-calling, the misunderstanding, the "Didn't you ride giraffes in Africa?" the "Did y'all have houses there?" the "Africans are too aggressive" the "Y'all Africans think you're better" the "Well, you don't look African" the "When I said that thing, I was talking about other Africans" the "Does anyone in your family do 409 scams?" the "Are you even American?" the "blue black" the "You sold us" the "damned Africans" the "Did they have multiple wives there?" the "Do you know voodoo?" the "Why is Africa so poor?" the "Why do Africans smell?" the "Mutombo" the "Grace Jones" the "*National Geographic*" the "*African Booty Scratcher*" the "You don't sound like a black person" the "My parents donate to Africa" the "black people are so sensitive" the overeager "YESS, girlfriend!" the "How did you know that?" the "Where did you go to school?" the "I'm not a racist, but" the "damned black people" the "But why do they have nice cars and live in the projects?" the "My mom didn't really mean that thing she said. You know how the older generation is" the "Did you get any help on this paper?" the "If you talk about being black too much, you're the racist" the "We won't be able to give you that promotion this time" the "I don't see color"—we took it all.

What I saw in the eyes of those first-generation Americans and young black immigrants like myself was the stress of never arriving, the impatience, the disconnect, the madness of identity. I admit I escaped, I whispered on a call to Johnny Boy, weeks after, when he was still calling to see if time had changed me. I did look for this home on the shoulders of love. I could not help it. That was my inheritance. But by spring, after fall, after Johnny Boy and those calls, when I made room for my thoughts, for myself, I knew I could no longer look for my reflection in the men I chose. And home, my first home, was the beating drum.

"Are you well?" Papa asked and his voice pulled me from the waves. I had called Mam's phone but he picked up, and I was better for it.

"I am," I answered softly.

"Mam says you got a dog," he said and I imagined him smiling.

"I did. A black Lab," I said.

"Hm. They are the best dogs," he said, then seemed to loiter in the silence, like those who were far better at showing their love than at navigating its words.

"Mam says you started working on your book again. That's good."

"Yeah, I'm trying," I said from my fire escape, the laptop and empty screen scrutinizing me from my desk. "Writing is hard. It can be hard, Daddy."

"Sure, but who better to do those kinds of things?" he asked in that steadfast way.

And there it was. His colossal being. His words pulling thunder from the sky.

"Thank you, Daddy," I said, my lips trembling in the silence. "For everything."

"I don't know what I did but I will take it," he laughed. "Here's your mom."

Mam said hello almost immediately, taking the phone to commence small talk and news of her day.

"How is . . ." she started to ask, finally.

"We're no longer seeing each other." I rushed to tell Mam before she could finish.

"Oh. Since when? He seemed nice," she blurted, but in stutters.

"He was. He was very nice. But . . ."

"How are you feeling?"

"I'm well, I'm good," I assured her. "This isn't like the last one."

"Okay," Mam said.

"I think I want to go back to Liberia," I blurted and waited to hear the slightest movement on the other end of the line.

"Well, are you sure? Dry season is almost over."

"I think so. I started having that dream again. About Satta," I said.

"Oh. Did you think about . . ."

"I did. And she was nice too. But I'm good. I want to do my own work," I said, remembering the vanilla smell of the therapist's office. Mam was silent for longer than I knew what to do with, so I sat on the sill and waited.

"I think it's time," I said in the void.

"Come then," Mam had said finally, as if conceding a fight she had long hoped she would lose. "Come home."

SEVENTEEN

I arrived at night. From the sky, Monrovia was a mass of blackness with the occasional pocket of light that looked no more significant than a colony of fireflies. Almost everyone in the plane sounded like Papa and Mam, and for that reason I felt safe. I thought I would experience fear or anxiousness, those friends who consumed much of my last memories in that city. But there was warmth, a victory in the landing, mild clapping in the cabin.

As I exited the plane and descended the stairs onto the tarmac, the smells of fresh rubber sap, fried greens, and sweat competed for my senses. I examined the faces and postures of those waiting on the ground for hints of familiarity. Words, both shouted and spoken quietly, clashed into each other as the airport workers hustled to accommodate and also size up the passengers of their latest flight.

I had been staring at a woman's freshly painted red nails and the neat fit of her uniform when she caught me.

"Welcome," she said, smiling as she searched my face and eyes to see if I was of any importance.

"Thank you," I whispered and hurried into customs.

I entered a small room with posters labeled "Liberian" and "Diplomat" and "Non-Citizens," which looked to have all at one point been white but were since stained by neglect, and noticed that a thin man wearing a T-shirt too big for his frame held a torn piece of paper with my name on it.

"Hi, Wayétu, welcome home," he said as soon as I read the sign. "Your Pa sent me for you."

I nodded and smiled, immediately following him as he processed my passport and led me to an area where the entire flight stood shoulder to shoulder, anxious for their bags to teeter across the broken ribs of an outdated carousel.

"How was your flight?" he asked, as though he knew me, content and committed to my comfort and happiness, as much as to delivering me to Papa and Mam without error.

"It was fine," I answered, as the carousel shifted, then reluctantly inched along.

"Don't worry," the man said, "just point out the bags to me. Your Ma and Pa waiting outside."

He rushed to grab my bags as soon as I pointed to them, squeezing his way between the unmethodical assembly. We exited the crowded room and airport, and a sea of black faces waited anxiously outside. There were Ankara and country cloth shirts and dresses on some of their bodies, the kind that Mam used to wear, while others wore light T-shirts and shorts to cope with the dry season humidity and Harmattan winds. Immediately, I realized that I was an entity for consideration. I was wearing jeans and sandals with a white blouse, and I wore my weave in a ponytail that hung down my back. People looked at my face, at my clothes and bags, as if I were an alien, before tiring of it all and searching beyond where I stood for the family member or friend who had not yet emerged.

The man led me past the initial group to the edge of the parking lot.

I recognized them in the distance, peering ahead as if waiting for a right answer in a mass of incorrectness, the only one that mattered.

They looked the same. Papa wore a polo shirt and fidgeted with his keys. He wore glasses now and they glared in the distance. Mam held her purse with both hands, her neck searching, her braids thin and neat.

There is a weight that builds on shoulders when one leaves home. The longer a person stays away, the heavier the burden of displacement. I saw Papa and Mam standing there and the lost hours returned, came back to me in layers. There were familiar intonations that gathered across the parking lot, those vowel-heavy words like an ocean pushing against me, those faces and bodies like mine, like my friends', and the burden lifted, died in that moment. Mam started toward me with her arms extended, crying, and I hurried to her, buried myself in the resurrecting cloud of her presence.

"There she is," Papa said and joined our embrace, his brooding body an extra sheet of nostalgia.

"Sorry," Mam said, crying over my shoulder, and I was not sure for what. My recent heartbreak? The long flight? We would talk longer, in private, she gestured this with a nod, and I took comfort in the fact that she had not changed. Papa paid the man sent in to help me, who by now had loaded the truck with my bags.

"Thank you, chief," he said, nodding, and scurried to another cluster of vehicles that had just arrived, hopeful for his next gig.

Our drive home was pitch black except for Papa's two beaming headlights on the dim road away from Robertsfield airport. I rolled down the window so those smells could awaken my memories—peanut soup, oil from dry fish, the rising smoke from charcoal pots. The night sky was so complete with constellations that I gasped. We navigated the dusty and bumpy roads in the darkness, and I saw clusters of palm trees, various congregations of *pen-pen* drivers, and moonlight markets of vendors selling coconut, corn, and other goods remaining from the day. I searched faces, scanned them as they filled the dirt junctures of those roads.

That night, Mam made my favorite dish. She served me cassava leaves over rice with deep-fried fish and pepper sauce, and as soon as the warm greens rested on my tongue, I was ashamed for having attempted to make the dish myself.

"You eat rice with a fork now?" Mam asked, as she and Papa filled their spoons.

I laughed with her and glanced at the polished, naked spoon she had placed beside my plate. I took another bite.

After dinner when Papa left the table, Mam held my hand to stay.

"How are you doing with . . . are you still dreaming?" she asked and coughed after she said it, placing a napkin over her mouth, so gracefully that I committed the moment to memory to learn the way.

"Better. It's only once in a while. But they're all similar now."

She leaned back in her chair, her posture perfect. She had already settled so well "back home" as they called it. So why did she let us call Texas home for so long, if she knew that hers was not the same?

"And how are you doing?" she asked, eyes locked with mine, in the soft way Mam smiles at her children, that enigmatic language, when she knows exactly how we feel.

"I'm well," I answered and mimicked her smile. But she knew better.

No matter how old and together I liked to think I was, sharing any space with my parents, and specifically Mam, who was the only person in my life who always seemed with me, and also always left me, exposed even the most subtle sensitivities.

"Tell me about Satta," I said finally. "I want to hear about her."

"There is nothing much to hear, dear," Mam said. "Her name was Satta Fahnbulleh and she was from a town called Weelor in Cape Mount. Satta fought for Charles Taylor, and she was maybe sixteen or seventeen years old. That's all I know."

"That's all?"

Mam shrugged. "Yes. Unfortunately. What else was there to know? We were all desperate."

"And there was no way of contacting her? No way to write her?"

"How?" Mam said, lines now spread across her forehead, as if I had already managed to overwhelm her, with just a few hours of time between us.

"Everything will be okay, Tutu. You're home now," she said after a brief silence. She stood up from her chair and kissed my cheek as if I was five again, and I was afraid and I longed for my mother, and we had not seen each other in a long time.

Before we reached the Vai Town bridge after SKD Boulevard, traffic had no king, and cars and trucks shared roads with *pen-pens* and *keh-kehs*—transport motorbikes and enclosed motorized tricycles—both of which Papa forbade me ever to ride.

"They can't drive. Those things are dangerous," he said.

"It'd be easier if the roads weren't so awful."

"Seriously," Mam agreed from the passenger seat.

They had both taken a few days off from the university for my homecoming.

"When will they fix them?" I asked, to which Papa huffed.

"Who knows," he answered, his hands steady on the wheel.

"And they've been this way since the war?"

"Most of them, yes. The rebels destroyed the infrastructure. Pulled out pipes and wires to go sell."

"Who ruins the thing they're fighting for?" I shook my head, disenchanted.

"Maybe Liberia is not what they were fighting for," he said in a low tone, and the words lingered for moments after, haunting me.

Those childhood images of princes marching into a vast and webbed forest—Kru princes and Mano princes and Congo princes. Indeed, Liberia was not the entire motive, the full story. And how could it be? In my classrooms in America, I cringed when we discussed African wars. I argued with a classmate once that America too had once had a civil war, on a day I struggled for words to defend African dignities and contest his claims that Africans were barbaric for always fighting.

But Papa was right that most Liberians, most, did not choose Liberia to be their country. Just as Ivorians did not choose. Just as Ghanaians and so many others did not choose; some men in Berlin in 1884 drew those lines, gave those names. Without agency, who can love a country forced upon them? Those princes from my childhood were fighting not only for their people but also for their nations, the countries they chose. Gio is a country. Mano is a country. Kpelle is a country. Vai is a country. And these nations were centuries old. Men and women across the continent would die with those nationhoods on their hearts. Out of the window, each journeying face a labyrinth I paced for hints of our former life, I melted at every dead end.

"Where did the rebels go?" I asked Papa, and watched as his hands squeezed the steering wheel.

"Look outside the window. They're all around here," he said. "Some of these taxi drivers, gas station attendants, security guards. They're everywhere."

"They just picked up and resumed their lives as if nothing happened," Mam said.

As Papa's truck snailed along a road riddled with potholes, Monrovia seemed to be thriving, bursting with movement. *Pen-pen* drivers crowded junctions beside markets where coconut, fried plantain, and fresh produce vendors chatted as customers searched their inventory. A man wearing a faded Cleveland Browns T-shirt paced behind three rows of church shoes, neatly polished, as a few customers loitered nearby, taking second looks at the shiny stock while waiting for the next taxi. There were Chiclet and Kleenex sellers, and men waving fresh fish from rank, overflowing buckets by their tables. There were preachers and mechanics and schoolteachers and pimps. Fortune-tellers and accountants and hustlers and caterers for hire. Weave salesmen and saleswomen—"Attachment! Attachment!" they screeched. The packets of straight and wavy, sporadically highlighted Malaysian hair were just like the kinds I would find in Korean-run beauty supply stores on Nostrand and Flatbush Avenues.

There were singing blind beggars, quotidian, and pop-up gas stations with merchandise sealed in glass mason jars and beer bottles, their prices handwritten neatly on cardboard beneath their stands. Bushmeat pushers dangling deer and other forest herbivores by their hind legs. Uniformed schoolgirls who held hands as they ran across the road, giggling, oblivious but self-aware, and it made me think of the Blackgirls in Texas, and wonder about the social order of Liberian lunchrooms.

Cars teetered along and taxi drivers swore out of opened windows with their last breaths.

"I don't remember these markets," I said.

"They were not here in NormalDay. Not like this," Papa said. "Not before the war, and certainly not before the coup. More and more people from all over the country moved to Monrovia for jobs after we left."

Cars honked around us, and every so often a black SUV raced ahead of the stagnant rows of cars. Some had portable flashing sirens on their hoods, some were followed or preceded by a few cars or *pen-pens*, and they created third or fourth lanes into oncoming traffic. The cars in the opposite lanes stopped or drove to the edge of the road, making room for the unvarying black vehicles and the men they carried.

"Are those cops?" I asked Papa, and he laughed.

"No. They're mostly politicians."

"Do you know any?" I asked, making a mental note to peer through the windows for what these men looked like.

"A few. But many of them didn't live in Monrovia when we were coming up."

I envisioned the men in those cars who were once children up-country in ignored villages—their families unable or uninspired to make the trip to Monrovia for lack of resources, of opportunity, of housing, of connections. Then after the 1980 coup, culminating with Liberia's wars, these families, many disregarded by the monopoly of power that existed in the city walls before then, moved en masse to live within Monrovia's borders, changing the face and shape of the city, reconstructing its body, an incurable metamorphosis. And these children grew up to buy the cars and the house staff and the girls, just like the men their fathers and grandfathers had once criticized. Tailored suits and bow ties. Security men and rubber farms. Gated homes and lawns too expansive for the children their wives let them claim as their own. I recalled the pictures I once saw of those first settlers in Monrovia from America, who wore top hats and three-piece suits during the dry season, on days that could not have been less than ninety degrees. But they had made it to a land, made it back home to the continent, free now with a country all their own. And they built the houses and the farms and the government, built the churches and the schools and the clinics, and they bought the clothes like the men their fathers and grandfathers had criticized. They say the master's tools can never dismantle the master's house. And alas, those at the soundless core of Liberia, then as well as now, tired of attempting to overthrow their rulers, use their master's tools to build houses of their own. To build cities of their own. And how? How does one model a nonpareil freedom with the master's tools, the same used to mold the institutions that kept them in chains? Pyrrhic victories.

An eager crowd ran toward an already overflowing taxi. One woman managed to squeeze in and the taxi faded out to a dirt road between two corner market sellers. Papa finally turned from the main road.

"Does this look familiar?" he asked when we arrived at a house with a tin roof and a full clothesline along the side of the structure. The green paint was chipped across the surface and half of the cement of the front porch was missing.

"What is this?" I asked, squinting at the overgrown bushes in the front yard.

"It's Caldwell."

The house, now small and unfamiliar, stood ruined, like an estranged friend, a friend who'd wronged me and still was anxious for me to make the first move. Mam's garden was gone, and the roof had been replaced with sheets of zinc. The once-paved roads of the neighborhood had been reduced to dirt and rocks—the road to the neighboring houses unrecognizable. Iguanas and lizards clambered over the outlying bushes and palm trees.

"Wow," I said, my voice cracking, and opened the car door.

"No," Papa said, almost shouting.

"Why? I want to ask to go inside."

"No. That somebody else house now."

"Wait, what? They're squatters. You own that house," I said closing the door.

A woman appeared on the porch wearing a lappa tied tightly to her waist, a child tied to her back.

"Let them have it. There is nothing in there for me. Not anymore."

After the port, after the game of dodging potholes, careful not to scrape the edges, as if each were a wide-open gate to the bellies of hell, we reached Vai Town. And half a mile beyond the port, before a gas station, there is a road once paved, now hunched and imploded, with shacks born of war on either side. I grew eager to reach the end of that road. I could not wait to see her.

"They won't win!" a man shouted, pointing to a television, crowded at the feet by young boys avoiding schoolwork or selling water packs in traffic to add to their family incomes.

"You a damn fool. You see they up like that you say they will not win? You think it easy thing, scoring in soccer?"

And beyond the salt of those words there was more road, more children playing, unaware of how those plum trees bloomed in NormalDay. And beyond those children, at the end of that Logan Town road, there sat a house underneath a plum tree, and an old woman on the porch. Frail she was, her full head covered, her neck almost gliding with the wind to turn her face toward the various subjects, as if they were all a part of her kingdom, as if they orbited around that house.

Before the car even stopped, I was undone with tears. I had been away for so long—in that new country—and how could I know she was waiting? Her wrinkles told time, told stories. Her corneas were rimmed with gray. I exited the car and she squinted, concerned.

"Ol' Ma," I said and stumbled up the porch steps. She still glared sternly at me, a stranger yet her kin.

"Ol' Ma," I said again. I touched her hands, my neck a canvas of tears, and they were still warm, still soft.

She looked at Mam, confused, then at me. After she repeated this, her arms stiffened, as if she had been jolted by lightning, and she squeezed my hands.

"Tutu!" she said, an ululation.

How many times had I thought about her while I was away? I had traded her language for friends who mispronounced my name, her stories for southern deference and suburban preteen angst. The smell of her foods, the way she pounded potato greens in that wooden pot, holding the pounding stick tightly with both hands at its crown, the dance of mothers come and gone, to make the harvest softer, easier to digest.

I held her hand. Would this heal the sourness of my dreams? Remember, she said, the sound of music, those songs about our childhood before the war, those romantic overtures, a reckoning. Remember, she said, you girls were like them, waving toward the children assembled for games in the open yard outside her gate. I was precocious, she said. I had run out into the field, she said. And while I cried, no matter how hard I cried, when she called my name I stopped, at once, because she said I seemed to know that tears were a way of letting the world know that the healing, the work, had already been done.

"*Uhn wa meh lugn,*" Ol' Ma said in Vai, and an aunty called for her nurse.

"Take her. She will take her," Papa said, gesturing my way to take my grandmother to her room.

"Oh. Okay," I said nervously. I quickly glanced between him and Mam, only then remembering my parents' warning, that the woman I remembered, so vibrant and young, our surrogate in my recollections of the war, could now barely walk on her own. I lifted her from her seat, and she gripped my wrists, firmly. She leaned backward, as if her body would collapse, or melt, and I pulled lightly. I drifted across the porch toward the front door, and my Ol' Ma hobbled beside me, her body shrunken with years, her head tie dangling from her shoulders. She who once sold her inherited lappas to be traded in Junde during the war so we could eat. She who carried me across those fields and now relied on my direction, my pace. I felt her breathing in my hands, in her grasp, every step an introspection of those months of running.

When I was a girl, I wanted only for the dreams to stop. I wanted white space in my sleep so that I did not jump when shadows arose from the stirring sun. I wanted that medicine man to cut the demons out of my mind—remnants of a past of images now parasites of my imagination. When the sounds of the night, no matter how sweet, how familiar, intruded, I crawled sobbing across the hall and hid between Mam and Papa as they slept. They pulled me close to them and sometimes Mam wept with me. They laid their hands on my forehead and pleaded my case to God as Mam's voice rifted and split open. Nothing worked.

One Sunday they told me the story of the beggar at the Siloam Pool—about how Jesus rubbed mud on his eyes and thereafter he could see. My teacher expressed concern about the stories I was writing in class—talking and running trees, houses with hands, singing dragons. Mam became afraid that year when she heard stories of American authorities taking children away from their homes if they were not cared for properly, and they could not afford therapy for me so sometimes while we played and she thought I was not looking, I saw her wipe her eyes during a deadlock gaze in my direction.

This blind beggar—it was his bath in the Siloam Pool that cleaned his eyes and restored his sight. I was just a girl, but I decided I would be baptized.

And Papa and Mam had gently pushed me to a pastor waiting in the water. I touched his hand as my bare feet got acquainted with the floor of the pool. The water was warm. It was the closest I had been to touching the cross behind the pulpit and I would have stretched out my hand but I knew that Papa would not be pleased.

"I now baptize you in the name of the Father and of the Son and of the Holy Spirit," the pastor said and sunk me into the pool.

Underneath the surface, my hands and feet extended to either side of me and I opened my eyes through the thick liquid haze. I came toward three ceiling lights in the distance and the water pushed against my skinny limbs and crept into me through hollows. That is the moment I should have thought of God and my healing, but instead I thought of my Ol' Ma. Mam told me Ol' Ma would never be baptized because she was Muslim, and as the pastor lifted me I was overwhelmed with sadness. I will never leave her behind, I thought.

"Never leave you behind," I whispered that night on the porch to my Ol' Ma as the iguanas cased Ol' Ma's steps and the laughter of Mam and her sisters resonated throughout Logan Town.

"What did you say?" Mam asked from across the porch, watching me still.

"Nothing," I answered.

Another lizard revealed itself from behind the leg of Papa's chair and scurried to the porch steps to the outlying yard.

"Another one!" I said. "Why are there so many? Geez."

"They're everywhere," Papa said.

"You know," Mam said, laughing, "one of my students told me the people here believe that the reason there are so many more lizards and iguanas now versus NormalDay is that they are the spirits of those lost during the war."

They laughed at the thought and continued talking, kept eating those peppered dishes into the evening, while children were relentless in their games beyond the gate. And I watched those lizards more closely now, tried to catch their eyes in their beats of rest and inquisition, when their bodies became still and their necks lengthened, looking for what? For whom? When the next one tarried near the porch gate, not far from where I sat, I extended my hand and it scampered away, hid in a bush, and something about the brush, the day, the words made me smile in its direction.

"Death is not the end," I thought I said to myself.

EIGHTEEN

"Agnes? Can you hear me?" I said on a call back to America a few days later.

For three years after the Second Liberian Civil War, which ended in 2003, a casual acquaintance, Agnes Fallah Kamara-Umunna, hosted a show called *Straight from the Heart* from a UN-sponsored radio station in Monrovia. She had visited a slum and found a shanty with fourteen former child soldiers she later interviewed, and thereafter she began to air the testimonies of victim rebels on her show. She gathered testimonies, interviewed victims and warlords, and even convinced some former child soldiers to testify at Truth and Reconciliation Commission hearings. She was the only person I knew who had access to the postwar rebel communities in Liberia.

"Yes, I can hear you," Agnes responded in that hybrid Sierra Leonean and Liberian accent.

"Good. Listen, Agnes, I'm in Liberia. I came back and I think . . . I think I'd like to find a rebel soldier. A woman."

"What?" she asked from what sounded like a moving car.

"Yes. One of Taylor's rebels," I said. "Her name is Satta. She was from Cape Mount, but that's all I know."

"I know too many with that name," she laughed. I tried to explain the story, though I knew I was unclear, stuttering. What was there to tell? Mam sent a woman to get us out of the war. I had come back. I wanted to find her.

"Listen, you should talk to somebody on the ground in Liberia. I can't help you," Agnes said, and instead convinced me to take the number of one of her contacts who would. "He is safe, don't worry," she said. Agnes convinced me that if he did not know Satta, he was the most likely person to know how I could find her.

After writing down the name and ending the call, I closed my notebook. For eight months my dreams had been seized by the image of that woman. A teenage girl, younger than I am now, a scarred, plain-clothes rebel, a gun slung over her shoulder, a jug of oil in her grasp—she came bearing gifts.

I opened my notebook again, transported to that moment in Lai as I gazed at the number. Agnes had given me the name of a man who fought during the First Liberian Civil War as a general under Prince Johnson's faction, INPFL. For a couple of days after getting the number, I hunted opportunities to tell Papa and Mam. I brought up our time in Lai more than usual, with a strong focus on the day Satta came.

"I told you everything I know," Mam sighed with exasperation. "Do you know how hard it will be to find a woman named Satta Fahnbulleh in Liberia? That's like looking for Maria Gonzalez in Mexico."

My parents grew impatient with my questions, and I found myself taking walks around the university's Fendell Campus, where they worked and had an apartment. Papa once casually mentioned that the security guards were mostly ex-rebels, and like a mosquito drawn to rainy season skin, I loitered near their stations in wonder. First I asked for directions to Papa's office in the engineering school. They smiled so widely it reduced their eyes to slits, they were courteous, friendly, all welcoming me to their neighborhood and spaces. The questions ballooned into suggestions for how to improve my colloqua, the Liberian pidgin that had become ruler in the mouths of the country's youth. By the third day, I walked to one of their stands at the side gate, where a man named Deek sat in an old wraparound school desk from six thirty in the morning to seven at night. Over the week, the conversations got longer each day, after I insisted to Mam that I'd stroll to Papa's office, or wanted to give Deek a bottle of water after we'd arrived home from a day of exploration and reunions. I had a bottle of water on the day that I finally decided to speak to him about the war.

"Hi there." I waved and he ran toward me, to lessen my effort.

"Hey Ma," he said, reaching me, a short and stocky man with dark skin and hopeful eyes. "You got something for me today?"

"Water again," I said, and stomached the disappointment that coated his eyes.

I offered chitchat about my day and his, and perhaps it was general anxiety about the question, or my intentions, but I blurted: "I want talk to you about the war."

"The war?" he asked, confused.

"Well, yeh. I've been trying to find a woman who was a rebel, and I heard maybe you knew some rebels." I tripped over the words, then quickly tried to front an ease, but it was too late. His eyes glazed over and at once the wall that stood between us was revealed as smoke, and the false hope that I could have such a conversation without an introduction, a caveat, as a foreigner, as he understood me, and any Liberian who spent the years I did away from home, punched my throat, and I was immediately sorry.

"Who you looking for?" Deek asked, placing his hands in his pocket, and my heart pounded and those dark memories returned in flashes.

"A woman who fought, but we will talk. We will talk," I said, turning quickly from him and returning to my parents' apartment, not looking back, although I heard him say "Okay" or "See you tomorrow, Ma" or "Thank you for the water" and I could not believe I was so daft, so foolish, so brazenly audacious. I dared not look back.

Inside the apartment, Mam was in the kitchen while Papa sat in the living room reading. He looked down at the book in his hand and rubbed the side of his head, in the way he did when he was not processing the words he read.

"Where did you go?" Papa asked, still looking at his book.

"To talk to Deek," I said, trying to be casual, indiscernible.

"Why?" Papa asked and looked up at me, but spoke before I could respond. "Your Mom says you looking for that woman? Why?"

"I . . . I don't know," I admitted. "Curious, I guess."

"Be careful," he said. "You hear me?"

"Yeh," I nodded aggressively. Those eyes of his, in that look he gave when he returned to the cavities of my dreams, and those months of running.

"The guns are still buried," he said, his eyes, true, still undone, digging into mine.

His voice was softer than I expected; he sounded reserved, forgiving of my oblivion and uncertainty. Before I could begin, Mam walked into the bedroom where I sat conducting the interview, startling me.

"Who are you talking to?" she whispered, a beautiful head peeking through the door frame.

"Someone who may know about . . . Satta," I answered quickly, then shook my hand and waved her away, mouthing that I'd tell her later. "*You girl, you crazy? Don't bring your American thing here,*" I was sure she would say with a stern, chastising tone and lecture about my safety during the visit.

After an unsuccessful attempt at small talk that likely unmasked my fear of the conversation and his history, I divulged details about my search for Satta, almost whispering, in the same way I had shared with Agnes. When I spat out the last word, I felt dizzy, as if I were dreaming that conversation and the circumstances around it.

"I know of some like that," he said after I spoke. "Even the worst of them, who were helping the people escape and cross the border."

"Wait, what? Really?"

"Oh yeah," he said. "Sometimes you know what they doing, you just turn your eye. Other times . . ."

It was an understood silence.

"I will help you," he said with ease.

I was taken aback by his generosity and wanted immediately to talk to Agnes about what he owed her that was so valuable that he was so willing to help me. In my right mind I perhaps would have hurried off the phone, but the same curiosity that birthed my search formed other words for the general, questions he welcomed, like why, and at times in the conversation, it seemed, missed. I learned he'd become a Church of God pastor, although he had no congregation. Rather than preaching, he began a rehabilitation ministry for former rebels addicted to cocaine, dujee, and by-products of crack. In a process he called "dry detox" initiated in 2007, young boys were asked to sign a form forfeiting their basic human rights for full immersion in his program. They then spent three days in a dark cell with a meal a day of beans and milk.

"It is spiritual," he said. "I want them to come out of the darkness physically, but I want them to come out spiritually too." And had they? After emerging from the first three days, the boys were tortured by withdrawal tremors; if the boys still did not escape, they were bathed with cold water and the counseling began.

The young bodies of the prince's soldiers danced in my memory— their invisible drums and the guns and lives they carried. Meanwhile, stories across the world went on. The general's, and those stretched across vast plains and always resurrecting cities of *the west*, and mine. God had forgiven him, he said, and that was enough. He did not answer to man but to God and that familiar litany, the song the guilty play on repeat.

After hanging up the phone, I sat unmoved on the edge of the bed, in silence. I was not sure what my exact expectations of the conversation were, but as I sat there I wanted more.

The air-conditioning wall unit sputtered from the surges of an unreliable generator, my parents' voices floated toward me in murmurs from the adjacent room, life moved about outside the window— laughing children, market women, students—and I sat in stillness.

Two days later the general called me with news that he did not find any woman who fought for his faction or others named Satta. Instead, he gave me contact information for two pastors who directed me to another woman named Agnes, each of whom said things very similar to the story I told them of Satta.

By now I had admitted to Mam what I had been up to, and after sucking her teeth at my foolishness, she then insisted my conversations were all to take place in her vicinity. I spoke to Agnes on a Tuesday afternoon, on a phone call in my parents' living room.

"Hi, hello," I said, smiling, looking at Mam, who sat on the living room sofa periodically glancing at the phone, as if it were the woman herself.

"Yeah, hello," she answered.

A thirty-eight-year-old wife and mother of four from Kakata, Liberia, Agnes had fought with the general and INPFL. As a young teenager, she joined his faction, not by force like many other girls who fought during that time, but out of obligation to her family.

"I did not have support," she said. "If I joined, I was promised protection and food for my family."

She killed almost immediately, but out of fear for her life, she remained with the rebel army. "I helped who I could," she said. During the war there were various checkpoints where rebels would line up civilians and ask where they were from and to which tribe they belonged. If the civilian or group was suspected to be from an opposing side, they were killed. To help civilian Liberians, Agnes and other women rebels, like Satta, made a habit of lying at checkpoints.

"They would ask the people where they were from and I would speak up and say they were my tribe or my family so the boys wouldn't kill them," she said. Agnes was lucky to have lived after saving dozens of people during her time with INPFL. According to her, there were many like herself and Satta during both wars.

There was a young girl who fought with her who, after realizing what Agnes was doing, tried to save some innocent families herself. "They lined up the family and were yelling at them that they were Krahn," Agnes explained. The girl, younger than her, spoke up and said they were distant cousins. "She begged them not to kill the people. She said they were Bassa." The rebels held the family overnight and on the following morning, after it was determined that the family was indeed Krahn, they stood the teenage girl with them and shot them all.

"The woman who was known most for this was B," Agnes said. "She lied and said people were family and friends during checkpoints and she helped plenty of them cross the border." The last Agnes had heard, B had escaped to Sierra Leone after rebels discovered her "crimes" and sought to kill her.

"And you have never heard of Satta?" I asked again, wondering if Satta was ever as fortunate as B, or if her sacrifice for my family was her last. The thought made me weak. "I don't think so, no," Agnes said. "But . . . but if you can meet me in town tomorrow, maybe I bring somebody with me to talk more about the war."

"Really?" I asked, eyes widening at Mam, who stopped what she was doing. She pointed to her chest and I nodded toward the gesture. I knew she would come.

"And we will send her the place," Mam added.

"I can text you where to meet us. That would be great."

I wondered if she also thought my search was absurd—if she thought I was wasteful for chasing someone many, like my parents, and even maybe she, believed no longer existed, crazy for ignoring the fact that some saints, even mine, will die.

"Okay," she said in a high-pitched voice.

Mam and I woke up early the next morning to beat traffic into town, where we told Agnes to meet us at a ground floor café. Papa insisted that his occasional driver, a bearded gray-haired man named Sumo who always wore a hat, would take us. On the drive there I kept looking over at Mam, who seemed as eager as I was to potentially find ourselves one step closer to Satta.

"I think I want to talk to Deek more," I told her.

"The guard?"

"Yeah, and others like him."

"Why?" she asked, shaking her head.

"I still don't know. Curiosity, intrigue, answers. How does anyone live with that kind of past on their shoulders?"

Mam shook her head again and shifted her gaze to the lives out-side the truck window. Mam and I arrived at the café and ordered a few pastries and tea, sitting near the window so Agnes and her con-tact would be able to see us. We could see Papa's truck and Sumo from where we sat; he watched and waited patiently, nodding toward us any time we looked his way. I sent a text: "We are here. Right near the en-trance," which was answered with "Ok. Coming."

Mam stared at me occasionally from a book she was reading. I caught her as I read from my notebook, particularly from notes I'd taken while talking to the general. I did not think I would have time to speak in depth with Deek, so I made notes of questions I would ask during my next visit. About an hour after, when we did not see or hear from Agnes, I texted her again: "How far are you?" This time I received no response.

"What did she say?"

I shook my head, and Mam's eyes returned to the pages of her book. So I called. No answer.

"You gave the correct location, right?" Mam asked some moments later.

"Yeah," I said.

I added more questions to the notebook, sporadically tapping my pencil on the corners of the pages. I looked out of the window at Sumo, at traffic now resembling yesterday's, at pedestrians on the early-morning road to see if one of them were her.

I went to the bathroom and returned. I ordered more tea, more croissants. Twice.

"We should head back," Mam said finally, close to noon. "I have work to do."

"Why? I think maybe she's in traffic. You know how it can be," I refuted.

Mam stood up.

"Come on, this is important. Just let me call again," I insisted.

"You now call plenty. You're wasting your time."

"You can leave me here," I said. "Sumo can take you to work and come back for me."

Mam sighed, reluctant. "Okay," she said finally. "I'm just going to pick up something from campus and we will be right back."

"Okay."

"Less than an hour—"

"Cool."

"—and when I come back we're going home. She will not have you just sitting around all day."

"Okay, that's fine."

She grabbed her book and her purse, and strolled out of the café to where Sumo waited. As they drove off, I became more obsessed with the faces of pedestrians. I studied each one, although I would not have known her if she were looking me in the face. I jotted down notes again, reviewing the questions I would ask. I texted: "Everything okay?" and called and called again. And as if the day had a vendetta, Mam and Sumo returned, my heart dropping when I noticed Papa's truck turn the corner.

Mam did not ask me questions on the drive home. She did not have to. When I climbed into the truck, she shook her head, in disappointment but also what seemed to be disgust at the missed appointment.

"This too is Liberia," she whispered in her corner, and I ignored it, kept gazing outward.

It was not until we entered the apartment that the sadness, the absurdity that I hoped to be reunited with this woman, hit me. That I wanted to see her again to touch her, to thank her, to understand myself. The gravity of that season, the breakups and contemplation and wanting, disassembled me.

"What?" Mam said, immediately rushing to me, and I kept warding her off, pushing her off my skin. "What? It's okay," she said and I wanted to throw something but also to be held by her. "It will be okay. Don't mind these people. What?" she insisted and I pulled away again. I did not want to be in her embrace, but to look her in the face, in her eyes as I cried.

"What?" Mam asked, her lips trembling now, about to break.

"Why did you leave?"

RAINY
SEASON

NINETEEN

When I tell them the story, I say that 1990 was the year I cried. I tell them all year I looked out of my window in New York City, and I cried because I could no longer hear their voices. I was twenty-eight years old when I left Liberia. When the semester ended in December 1989, I returned to Caldwell while I was on vacation from school, and went back to New York only two short weeks later. I wore only dresses then, country cloth to Ankara. Sometimes, I let the girls wipe the lipstick from my lips with their fingers and rub it across their own. They did that the morning I left, taking turns smearing that serious color. I promised them that I would see them again during the rainy season in June when I was on vacation from school.

I arrived in New York, and the weather was so different from our Liberian dry season that my teeth clattered. I cried during the entire flight, rubbing my fingers against their pictures under the lamp of my window seat. When I tell them the story, I tell them that by the time I landed, my eyes were red and after exiting customs, I ran into a taxi. New Year's Eve was a few short days away so the streets in Harlem were busy with tourists. I had lived in New York for five months then, with another Fulbright from Japan named Yasuka, and an American woman named Anne, but when I got back to the apartment, they were not there. The silence made it even colder, and it was so cold that night I did not even unpack. I took off my shoes and climbed into bed, covering my body with sheets and blanket to keep warm. When that still felt too cold, and the bite of it reminded me of my sadness, I thought of him—Gus. I thought of my daughters and wondered what they were eating, if Korkor and Torma were helping them with their lessons, if they were happy. My thoughts were not peppered with their memory, they did not peek around the corners of my mind during the day; it was their ever-present memory that was seasoned with my thoughts, so that when I finished deciding whether I would wipe my eyes before falling asleep, or briefly wondered what I would do the following day, they were still there, never leaving my mind.

Ol' Ma says it takes a special man, a good man, to give his wife a blessing to leave him. That is what Gus did for me. I wanted to study in America, where I imagined everyone lived in buildings as tall as clouds, from Gus's stories of the few months he moved here shortly after the coup, and he told me I should come. Ol' Ma said that these special men are clever and confident, so confident that they trust their choice of women, and they would never choose women who would not return to them. So when I received the letter stating that I had won the Fulbright scholarship, Gus, in his specialness, encouraged me to go.

"You are right. You can't say no to the Fulbright. And at Columbia. In America!" he said, picking me up and dancing around the den, holding me close.

My Ma and Pa threw me a party at their house in Logan Town. I am the youngest of five girls and I have more cousins than I can count, so the house was crowded with familiar faces. Ma was known for her cooking and news spread that I would leave soon. I liked Logan Town most then, when guests filled even the yard around the plum tree. I spoke to Ma in the kitchen that day, stroking her hands as my girls played with the curtains in the corner.

"People are talking," I told her.

"About what?" Ol' Ma asked.

"That I have no business going to America when I have a husband and three daughters. They're saying he makes enough money and there is no need for me to go."

Ma made a deep sound, the sort of sigh she gave to ward off the enemies of her daughters, no matter how many rivers away.

"It's a master's degree, Ma," I said. "I can come back and do plenty with it. Maybe one day I can even work at the education ministry. Can you imagine?"

My Ma had told me that she was happy that we had all listened to her and gotten jobs and an education, no matter how well our husbands did.

She asked me about Gus and I looked across the house to her sitting room, where he sat with a group of men, holding a Malta. He was the first and only man I had ever loved. We married while we were still at the University of Liberia and started having children right away. First Wi, then Tutu, then K. He was a special man—I knew what Ol' Ma said was true—and even if I were to tell him that I wanted to move to Russia or to Vietnam or to Iceland, places too far away, if he knew those things would make me happy, he would have said yes.

The airport was busy and loud when he told me goodbye. He did not want me to miss my flight, so he rushed me. He was nervous, and I could tell because he acted the same way when he was watching a very important football game and Oppong Weah or another player he rooted for was going to lose.

"Make sure you read to the girls in the night," I said, stopping at the gate.

"If one of them gets sick, you call me, yeh? Even if it's just a cough, call me. Visit the Ol' Ma's house when you have time. They still want to see you. She says she will come visit plenty and help you with the girls. And be careful what you eat now that I'm not here. Don't get sick. You get sick this time, I won't be here to make pepper soup. You won't have my pepper soup and you will have to drink some other dry thing with no taste. You better call me, yeh? Anyway, if you don't call me, I will call you."

I looked into his face and he looked like he was waiting for me to cry, because that is all I had been doing that day. He hugged me and told me that he would be all right with the girls in Liberia, and that I could trust him. But I did not cry then. I looked into his face, that nervousness now trapped. Before I could say anything else, he wrapped his arms around my shoulder and squeezed.

"I love you, yeh?" I said in his ear, and I hugged each of my daughters, pulling them in.

My sadness was there also, and the same nervousness as his, but I kissed his cheek and hugged him tightly.

"Bye, Mam," he said, and those would be the last words I heard from him for some time. They watched my plane until they could no longer see it—a container to my weeping, my regret.

TWENTY

"Mam." I heard a low voice outside my bedroom door, followed by a series of knocks.

I sat up in bed and lifted the drapes of my window to let in some light. But it was cold there, so my drapes never stayed opened for long.

"Happy New Year, roomie," Yasuka, my roommate, said, smiling when I opened the door. She always brought me tea, so when we saw each other for the first time that year, she carried a tea set on a tray.

I let Yasuka into my room and returned to my bed to lie down. Yasuka, also an international student at Teachers College, was my closest friend. Yasuka left to visit her family in Japan on the same day I left for Liberia. She was my height and shared my slender build, my sense of humor, and my love of rice. We studied together, ate together, and the only time I didn't care for her was when I had to pull leftover strands of Yasuka's long black hair out of the bathroom drain so I would not have to shower in a puddle.

"What did you do for New Year's Eve?" she asked me.

"Nothing," I said. "I haven't been feeling well since getting back."

"That was a week ago!" Yasuka asked.

"Just a bit homesick," I said. Yasuka was clumsy at responding to sadness, so in the first days she got back to America, we spent a lot of time in silence. She took care of me, and made sure I had medicine. She did things like tie the drapes with a string on the sill, so that the sunlight could fill the room.

"It was good to be home," Yasuka said. "I miss my family too. They are proud of me, like your family, and your daughters are proud of you. They want you here to finish," Yasuka said. I appreciated her words and encouragement.

"Any news about your president?" Yasuka asked, drinking from her cup.

"It's still the same," I said, and my head ached to think about it. "The president does not want to step down and they say rebels are coming to remove him. But my husband says it will be quick and everything will be back to normal."

"When will you go back again?" Yasuka asked.

"During rainy season. Summer. June," I said.

"That's good!" Yasuka said cheerfully. "It will come soon. You will see."

I changed the subject to talk about school, and I always did this when my body became cold from the thoughts of war. We talked about the program, classmates we were looking forward to seeing when school resumed the following week, how we would use our degrees to affect our countries. There were so many words that I wanted to share instead of what we spoke of, things I was afraid of, thoughts creeping in dark corners, waiting quietly for their time.

The city was less and less foreign to me each day. I would visit the Statue of Liberty, the Twin Towers, and Carnegie Hall. I liked New York, although everyone seemed to move quickly here, fighting the concrete for time and money. Passing faces on the street, I would imagine the homes they had come from, the daughters they were going to see, to read to, the aging mothers to whom they had just fed soup.

What I liked least about the city was that, although I spoke English, people acted as if they did not understand me. I eventually learned to speak slowly, becoming patient, so that people would understand.

"You must not lose yourself there, that's all," Ma had told me before I left. "Look into your mirror in the night and when you start seeing you not the same, come home."

I did look different, but I felt different after that December visit.

It was in New York that I first felt invisible, as if nobody could see me. People did not look at my neck or eyes as they did in Monrovia. Outside my classrooms I was hardly looked in the eye. People in New York walked like they were in a dream. When I was out at restaurants with classmates who were white, waiters talked to my classmates before they talked to me. And if I went to the store with a white friend to look for something, the person at the store always spoke to the white person first, and it made me feel small.

"What is a white person?" my daughter asked once on the phone.

"A person with pale skin," I said. "Like Ms. Walters."

Ms. Walters went to our church in Caldwell. The girls were in disbelief that she was white when I told them.

"How your series coming along?" Gus would ask me during our weekly calls.

"I na speaking series-oh," I joked. "And if you just saw the way the people look at me when I open my mouth, hmph. Like I did something wrong."

During our calls, I wished the phone handle was his hand.

"Don't let it bother you," Gus said.

"I'm trying," I said. "How the girls?"

"They fine," he said proudly. "Torma doing well with them."

"I knew she would."

"And Tutu-geh will turn five next month and she say she want big party," he said.

"Give it to her. An April party will be beautiful. Invite everybody," I said.

"You all right?" Papa asked.

"I'm still not feeling like myself since Christmas," I said. "Sometimes I want to just pack my bags and come back home." This was an admission. When I tell them the story, I tell them that the only thing that made me stay was wanting my daughters to know that they could go after anything they wanted, that they could fly too.

"That's nonsense," he said. "You almost finished with your first year. June three months away."

"Yeh."

"If it continue, then go see doctor," he said.

"I will." I had promised him I would stop worrying about the rumors of war. There was nothing about Liberia on television, so during every call I asked questions. What is the latest? Has Doe stepped down yet to avoid trouble? Do you think the rebels will be successful? What will happen to you all? Have you thought of the worst-case scenario? Shouldn't we talk about what we will do? How many rebels will it take to remove him if they are serious? And how long? Will his soldiers put up a fight? And what will happen to the children? How are you explaining all this news to the girls? He ended up telling me that I was worrying myself too much, and that we should not talk about the war at all.

"Just worry about finishing there and coming home," he had said.

So when our conversation became silent and all I could hear was the sound of breathing, I hoped he knew what I wanted to ask.

"All is well, Mam," he said. "Just finish there and come back to us."

TWENTY-ONE

One Sunday in April before a study session, I visited Calvary Baptist Church on Fifty-Seventh Street with Yasuka, to hear a missionary speak on his travels to Liberia. I heard about the church from a friend at Columbia and was happy to have found a Baptist church where I could go talk to God. I wanted to get a good seat that day to ask questions, but made sure to sit at the end of the pew in case I became dizzy. It had been four months since my Christmas visit and I had not been able to shake the ill feeling I had since returning to New York.

Calvary was a marble building with two stories of red pews to seat its many members. The back of each pew had wooden compartments where hymnals were kept. From habit, I ran my fingers over the edges of the hymnal covers. When the presenter approached the stage, I smiled. My best friends lived in Connecticut. They moved from Liberia earlier in the eighties with their husbands, and I tried to see them once a month. They occasionally drove to New York to pick me up for lunch, or I took a train at Penn Station to go out and see them. Still, I was always happy to meet anyone who had been to Liberia. I missed it more than I ever imagined I would. I missed my family. I missed my rose garden and my living room, the couches I had carefully designed and had upholstered with a fabric my daughters helped me pick.

The presenter approached the stage and introduced himself.

"I want to speak to you about my travels, and also to share my experiences in a country that is much different from ours," he said.

The lights were dimmed and an overhead projector was turned on. The presenter clicked a remote and a picture of a young child, no more than four years old, black, dirty, naked against a wooded background, faded onto the screen. He showed several other pictures of children, similar to the first, appearing hungry, sad, some crying, all of them staring directly into the camera. He spoke of how difficult it was for him to find a single person who could read or write. At that point I started to sweat. He spoke of the lack of compassion among fathers, Liberian fathers, and what it said of the African men he had been around. I thought of my husband and my head pounded. Each picture made me feel nauseated—my body both hot and cold. Where was my garden in these pictures? Where was my husband and men like him? Where were my daughters?

"You have to say something," Yasuka said. "You must say something."

"When he is finished," I said, feeling more and more sick as the presentation went on.

He mocked the smells, pitied the schools, warned everyone there about setting foot on Liberian soil without good health. He showed many poor villages, burst-open sewers, and too many children sitting alone—more than I could count—who were without even half a cup of river water to wash their faces. An hour later, after turning off his overhead projector, when the last child in his picture was now free to dress and go on about his business, an offering was taken for the presenter and his family. The baskets filled with American dollars and a line formed to speak to him. He did not show the Liberia I knew and loved, but the pictures made me afraid. It was the worst version of the country I had ever seen, but this version, I feared, could be what Liberia could become with war. I went to him slowly, rehearsing what I would say. Yasuka walked beside me, annoyed and still noticeably angered by the presentation. Every few minutes she shook her head and looked at me. When we finally arrived at the front of the line, the presenter smiled and extended his hand. Yasuka shook her head at him but I took his hand.

"I just want you to know that I am from Liberia," I said. An assistant at his side handed pamphlets to us. Yasuka shook her head and looked away and I took the pamphlet. "This is very, very offensive," I said, raising my voice. The presenter stopped smiling. "I am very offended," I continued, but before I could say all that I had rehearsed in line, my body grew warm. I rushed out of the sanctuary and through the hallway to the nearest bathroom, where I quickly pushed open a stall and vomited—heaved all I had eaten that morning and everything from the previous day.

"Hello?"

"What happened? I've been so worried," I tried not to shout that night. My roommates were still asleep. It was morning in Liberia and the middle of the night in New York. "I've been trying to call every day after you missed last week's call."

"I know, I know, sorry," he said. "The people say the phone lines them spoiled." He sounded hasty and it worried me, but I was happy to hear his voice.

"I have so much to tell you. I went to Calvary last weekend and this man—"

"Mam—the phone is breaking. Mam?"

"Hello? Hello, Gus?" I shouted. I would apologize to my roommates in the morning.

"Okay, I can hear you," he said.

"Good. I know it won't last long then, enneh? Did the girls get the shirts I sent?" I asked.

"They did," he answered.

"Oh good," I said, missing his scent.

"I am going to go see a doctor. There is something wrong, I just don't know what. I thought maybe I was pregnant but I've been menstruating. It's light but there's still something," I told him.

"Be sure to let me know what happens," he said. It was late and I was sleepy, and I knew he would say that he had to go soon, but I wanted to sit there a bit longer.

"The Chens left," he said.

"What? Why?"

"They scared. The rebels still here and they scared. He say they will be back when things settle down."

The end of his sentence was broken, and the line was full of static.

"I love you, Mam." I heard that clearly.

I left Harlem early one morning with only one hard-boiled egg in my stomach. My stomach began to cramp and bend, and I was not sure if it was because the egg did not suffice or if I was suffering the same discomfort that finally led me to set an appointment.

In the waiting room I read the outside of a pamphlet held by the woman in front of me. I was alone again with my uncertainty. My friend Rose had called me the night before to tell me of a cousin who had recently left Liberia and made it to safety, calling her from Sierra Leone. "He said the people now start fighting," Rose had said. "Have you spoken to Gus?"

"Not for two weeks," I had told her. "I can't reach him."

She told me not to worry, as everyone seemed to be doing lately, as if Liberia's worst-case scenario had not finally come.

"Mrs. Moore?" I heard.

I walked toward a woman with blue-rimmed glasses and large dramatic curls, who looked more like she belonged in an optical ad than in that office. It was a standard "woman's clinic" room—curtain, armchair, posters, white counter with gloves.

"Everything will be fine," she said before leaving me alone. I undressed and lay on my back in the chair, waiting for the doctor.

"Mrs. Moore?" The doctor entered the room, followed by the nurse.

"Hello," I said.

"So you haven't been well," he said. "We're going to take some basic blood work but I'm going to get an ultrasound just in case. How regular have your cycles been?"

"They have been light," I said. "But they've come."

"Okay, well, let's get you set up here. You can relax. It'll be over before you know it." He smiled and proceeded to inquire about my health and family history. He told me to lean back, and everything seemed to be going well after he began, but then his hand stiffened.

"Everything all right?" I asked.

The nurse kept writing in my file.

"Well, Mrs. Moore, it looks like there's a baby in there."

"What?!" I asked.

"You see the screen?" he asked.

I saw the baby's head. It was perfect.

"You're going to be a mother again," he said, smiling, and my eyes swelled. I imagined the faces of my daughters, and how they would react once they found out.

"Light bleeding happens in some pregnant women, usually when the fetus has trouble attaching to the uterine wall."

"Is the baby okay?"

"We'll continue to monitor you, but it looks like it. Just continue to take care of yourself."

He may have explained things further. I may have thanked him. I must have shaken his hand and taken a business card from the nurse. I sat alone in the room. I felt alone in the world, having not heard from Gus and the girls for two weeks, and I cried.

TWENTY-TWO

I was not able to return to Liberia in June during rainy season as I had promised. By July there were no planes flying in or out of the country. Instead, I moved into a small apartment through on-campus family housing and spent my days and nights waiting by the phone in hopes of a call from Gus, or news that they were safe. A month had passed since I had heard his voice. When I tell them the story, I tell them that I watched news stations to catch clips of the conflict—hoping to see someone I recognized. The phone rang, but the calls were always from family and friends in America sending their prayers my way or asking whether I knew where they were. During the day I sat facing the window beside an air conditioner my super gave me. I tried to read, to study, but I could not. I tried watching television but the happiness on the faces of the characters made me sob. How could they smile so widely? How could they not know that people were dying?

I was afraid to go outside because I did not want to miss a call and barely left my living room. Yasuka had gone away for the summer, as had many of my classmates. I spoke to Rose and Masnoh frequently, though quickly, afraid I would miss a call from Liberia if I remained on the phone for too long. Eventually I moved my dresser into the living room so that I could stay close to the phone at all times. I laid my sheets and blankets on the living room couch, and on the days that were not so miserable I read the books spread across the floor, because I had to remind myself that I was still in school, and that when I saw my daughters again, I wanted to tell them that I had fought.

I wondered what they were doing—what they had been eating. I paced my living room floor, as my stomach finally grew in front of me. On those lonely June nights while I was wrapped in the laughter of children playing outside, the fire hydrants loud as they burst, the only way to deal with my worry was to dream of them.

It was in July and I was in the bathroom. I was looking into a mirror at a face that was more and more plump each day when the phone rang. I ran as quickly as I could into the living room, nearly stumbling over my feet.

"Hello? Hello, hello?" I asked, trembling.

"Mam! Mam!" said a familiar voice. "It's me, Facia."

I fell to the living room floor at the sound of my sister's voice.

"Facia! You are safe! Where are you?"

"I am at the airport. I made it to New York. I'm at LaGuardia. There was no way to call until now—"

"You here?" I asked, searching my immediate surrounding for my shoes.

"I here. I here with Bom."

"American Airlines?"

"American!"

"I coming, Facia!" I grabbed my purse and hurried out the door, hailing the first taxi that drove past.

"LaGuardia," I yelled. "American Airlines!"

It was a warm day and the taxi windows were rolled down. I laughed into the sun, then cried at the memory of Facia's voice, so recent, so familiar. I saw myself in the driver's rearview mirror, the darkened circles around my eyes. I used my fingers to comb my hair, then held my stomach until we reached the airport. I rushed out of the taxi. The terminal was crowded and I searched each face that passed for Facia's. None was hers. I ran through the terminal until I finally arrived at the room with bags. Through a crowd I saw my sister sitting on a bench, looking toward a glass overlooking the road, as beautiful as I had last seen her in December.

"Facia!" I shouted, nearly choking on my tears. We crashed into each other. In that moment, we were all we knew we had.

"You are pregnant," Facia said, looking down at my stomach. Facia, thirty-one years old at the time, wiped my face as if she were Ol' Ma. "Don't cry, Mam," Facia said, unable to heed her own words. "I am here now."

We stood for a long time, hugging, crying, some travelers looking on at the spectacle as they passed.

It was morning when the rebels reached Logan Town, where Ol' Pa and my sisters Alice and Facia were staying with others, including Alice's young son, Bom. There was shooting on the road and Ol' Pa made them go and pack their things.

"We will go to Lai," he said.

"And what about Ol' Ma?" Alice had asked, shaken by the guns in the distance.

"We will go to Caldwell first to get them?"

"We will go to Lai. She with Gus. He will make sure they get to Lai safely."

Facia and Alice had packed a few of their things.

On the front porch in Logan Town, they said Ol' Pa spoke to a neighbor, an older man who did not live far from their home. His jeep was parked outside as he spoke, and young children peered out of the window. Ol' Pa hurried inside and the man remained outside on the porch.

"Alice!" he called. "Come go with him."

Alice ran to Ol' Pa. Bom went to her and stood beside her. He was a thin boy, orange-brown and tall for twelve years old.

"The man says he's going to the airport. They are airlifting American citizens. They will take Bom," he said, looking down at his grandson. "He needs a guardian. You can go too."

"But what about Ma?" Alice asked, wiping her face, yelling.

"What about you? It is not safe here, Alice," Ol' Pa said, and looked at the man waiting on the porch.

"And what about you, Ol' Pa?" Alice asked, still shaking.

"Do not worry about me. Me, I'm going to Lai," he said. He towered over them—tall and majestic in his stature.

"No, no. You and Ol' Ma," Alice said, shaking her head. "You are old. Facia!"

Facia rushed to where they were standing.

"The man says they will airlift Americans, and Bom needs a guardian," she began and was unable to finish. Her tears filled her palms and Facia hugged her, letting Alice lean into her. Facia said they kissed each other more times than she could count, as only my sisters would.

"Hurry, he will leave soon," Ol' Pa said in a panic. The shooting sounded closer by the minute. He returned to the foyer, where he hugged and kissed Bom. Facia and Alice went to their rooms to collect traveling papers and other information for the embassy.

"Take care of your aunty, big boy," Ol' Pa said.

Facia hugged Ol' Pa as if she were five years old again. She sobbed into his chest.

"Come, come now," Ol' Pa said. "This will be over soon. Go to New York. You have Mam's number?"

"Yes," Facia said.

"And you have your papers?"

Facia nodded.

"Then go and come back in time for Christmas." His smile was hers.

Facia took Bom's hand and they ran into the man's jeep. In the rearview mirror, through the dust made by those running on the road, she saw Ol' Pa and Alice stand together on the porch, crying and waving until they disappeared.

I made Facia and Bom pepper soup. Stirred the water and tomato sauce and peppers and fish and bouillon and onions and salt into the pot with all my love. I watched as they drank, gripping their spoons as they sat together on my living room couch, still rattled from their journey.

"I should be feeding you," Facia said, and I could not stop crying. "Aye, Mam."

"It's just that I thought everyone was—I didn't hear from anyone for so long," I finally admitted.

"I can't imagine," Facia said.

"Before coming, you said you heard nothing from them?" I asked again.

"Everybody was running and rushing. Pa called and called but nobody in Caldwell picked up. He say Gus will take care of them. He say they will go to Lai until the war stop."

"But Caldwell so far from Cape Mount. So far from Lai," I said.

"Just pray," Facia told me.

Facia was able to come with Bom to America as his guardian, someone who could take care of him because Alice was far away. There were still American citizens in Liberia who were being airlifted to safety. Liberians tried their luck crossing into Guinea, Ghana, and Sierra Leone as men fought over who would be the next king.

"Sam Doe is saying he will not step down," Facia said after drinking her soup. "The rebels them all over Liberia just like roaches, spoiling everything trying to force him out of the presidency."

"What?"

"Buildings, cars, even pipes. They're digging up pipes to go sell. Destroying everything until he leaves."

I imagined the Liberia I had left—the sprawling beaches, the roads bending into markets.

On Saturday mornings in Liberia, I woke up my girls with music. With Miriam Makeba, Sunny Okosun, and Ladysmith Black Mambazo, Mary Kiazolu, and George Gozi. On Saturday mornings I would play these singers, these magicians, and dance to them while I cooked in my Caldwell kitchen.

"Pata Pata," one of Makeba's most popular works, was only one of a collection of around fifty songs that embedded themselves into the mold of that house. I danced there. I moved my feet and hips as though I were a part of the music. My girls rolled their pelvises around, then jerked their bottoms back and forth. I could still hear their laughter. Gus would sometimes join me, and they watched us, each step bringing us closer to Liberia's full story, the dancing and funky hiccupping beats that moved the junctions of their bones. The merging cultures and origins, all trying to make sense of a place they all wanted to call home.

That night I pressed Play on an old tape player, and inside there was a Miriam Makeba cassette. Makeba sang "Suliram," a song she recorded in 1960, an Indonesian lullaby whose title means "go to sleep." The song floated through the walls of my apartment and over me as I lay on my couch beside the phone and looked up at the ridged ceiling.

"*Suliram, ram, ram,*" Makeba sang as I cried. "*Suliram yang manis.*" The lyrics weighed me down. "Go to sleep," Makeba sang. But I could not. I walked to my bed, where Facia slept beside Bom, in the dark.

"You sleeping?" I asked, as if we were children, little girls again at Ol' Ma's house in Logan Town.

"No," Facia said, sniffing.

I found my sister's hand and held it. "*Suliram, ram, ram. Suliram yang manis,*" Makeba sang. And I swore I heard Facia sing along, hum and wail those prayers in the night, just as our mother would.

TWENTY-THREE

My baby was due at the end of September and my second school year had just begun. With Facia and Bom in the apartment I was more comfortable leaving, and I questioned them about phone calls as soon as I got home. Facia had found a job to help with the living expenses my scholarship could not cover. I had trouble paying attention in class, and if anyone asked me about Liberia or my family, I tiptoed around the truth, careful not to step on broken glass.

I had not heard from them since May, and Facia and I had no way of knowing where anyone was or if the family in Logan Town had all successfully made it to Lai. On September 9, a BBC news desk reported that Johnson had wounded and captured Doe and had declared himself president until elections could be held. Not even one week later, Prince Johnson and Charles Taylor were now fighting against each other. Prince Johnson ordered his men to seize the rest of Monrovia at all cost, even if it meant leveling the city.

When I was not at class I was in my apartment, the telephone an arm's length away. I hoped the baby would wait just a little while until the war outside was over, so his father would not miss his birth.

On a Thursday morning while I waddled and paced around the

rooms of the apartment to the accompaniment of CNN, the phone rang.

"Hello?" I asked, out of breath after rushing to the phone.

"Hello? Hello, Mam?" I was asked. There was static, white noise on the other side.

"Hello?" I yelled into the phone. "Can you hear me?"

The white noise continued but I held the phone close to my face, refusing to hang up.

"Hello?" I yelled again.

"Hello?" I heard again, and the white noise quieted.

"Who is this?" I asked, unable to recognize the voice.

"Amos. This Amos," he said.

"Amos?!" I yelled. "Oh my! Hi! How are you?! Where are you?!"

"I'm in Ghana. I was able to leave Liberia," he said with a wide relief that I could hear in his voice.

I was happy for him, yet his voice was like the prick of a needle. I looked down at my stomach.

"Oh, God bless you, Amos. Thank you for calling. I am well."

"Thank you, thank you," he said. "But that is not why I am calling."

My heart dropped.

"What?" Facia asked.

"What is it, Amos? What's wrong?"

"I called around for weeks to find you. Once I arrived in Ghana. I called family around America looking for Liberians in New York, then when I found Liberians in New York I had to find someone who knew people at Columbia. I am so happy I found you."

"Amos, what is wrong?" I asked again.

"Gus is alive. I know there is no way you can know so I wanted to make sure I told you."

I screamed into the phone and raised my hands toward the ceiling.

"They're alive," I repeated, crying to Facia.

"He saved my life, Mam. Rebel almost kill me and Gus gave him money to let me go. I walked with them first but we parted. They were going to Lai. I believe they made it."

"They in Lai," I said, now laughing.

"Praise God," Facia said and danced around the apartment.

The white noise returned and I thanked Amos through the haze. I was getting ready to hang up the phone when on the other side I heard Amos asking me to wait.

"Amos? Amos, I am still here," I said.

"I am sorry, Mam. But I must tell you there are some rumors I have been hearing from people who escaped from the Cape Mount area," he said.

"What? What rumor you hear?" I asked.

"They are saying Charles Freeman, the Ol' Pa, is dead. That he was killed. He was looking for food in Burma and the rebels them mistook him for a Mandingo leader and shot him. The Ol' Pa is dead. They say he was killed."

That a day could be so bittersweet. That a day could be so cynical. That life could be so cruel, so vicious. I dropped the phone and tilted my head back. I clenched my dress, unable to breathe, and I screamed into the morning, screamed from my depths, from the ends of my fingers, screamed into the morning that a day could be so merciless, that a year could be so cold. Screamed into the morning until I had nothing left.

TWENTY-FOUR

The griots and the djelis do not write down their stories. They are divine tellers with memories that span thousands of years of our history. They never needed to write. Their memories are scripture. They tell the Ol' Mas all that is and all that ever was and, on some occasions, what will be. Those Ol' Mas tell their grandchildren, and when those grandchildren become Ol' Mas, they tell their grandchildren, and when these grandchildren become Ol' Mas, they tell their grandchildren, and so on. This is how we recite scripture. This is how the truth was kept, how some decisions were made, and so I paid attention when the Ol' Mas told stories they had heard from their griots and djelis.

For instance, they said that you can tell a lot about what is to come by your dreams, and by the way your unborn child enters the world. If you dream of snakes, it means that someone will soon die. If you dream of water, a lake or the ocean, it means that someone will soon give birth. If children are not born crying, they will give much trouble when they get older. If children are born feet first, if they somehow manage to stand upright inside their mothers, then a battle is coming, and the mothers will win.

These superstitions lived on even with the growth of Christianity—children chewing bones in their sleep to wish death to a parent, thrusting a special dust on enemies to give them leprosy—all possible, even under a Christian God. So when the doctors told me that I would need a C-section, my first, showing me the image of my son standing upright inside me, it made me smile. It was the first time I had smiled in weeks, since the rumors of Ol' Pa's death reached us. I considered everything about Amos's call. His raspy voice, as though he had also been crying for longer than anyone should, stirring all that good news with the bad.

That year had made me cynical, but I still believed that everything had meaning. The call I received, the call I had been waiting for, came from a man who would have been killed had it not been for Gus. And whatever circumstance led to them being on that dusty road on that day, at that time, whatever stroke of luck made the encounter with that rebel go as it did, it happened, and I understood it to be a direct act of God, having meaning beyond what I could understand.

These things were reminders of my smallness and the many ways life functioned outside my control; but there were those coincidences that gave me a glimpse, though I was small, of just how powerful I could be. And I wanted to tell my daughters this. I wanted to teach them their power and remind them of it every day I could, especially during the seasons they felt small. I wanted to see them grow to be mothers themselves. I wanted to see them fall in love. I wanted to be there when they graduated from school. I wanted to make them soup when they cried, and to tell them sorry I was not there.

They said my son was standing inside me, that he had chosen to straighten his back before entering what was then the coldest world, and I thought of those lives in Liberia. The griots and djelis would say that something was to come, that a battle was approaching beyond moons, that all of these things were the answer I had been praying for. So as the anesthesia entered my bloodstream and the ceiling lights blinded my eyes to closing, I thought of Liberia, my home, now a battleground calling for my return.

TWENTY-FIVE

Roy's office was in the basement of Teachers College at Columbia. I met him when I was only in middle school—he had come to Liberia with the Peace Corps and taught me social studies. He made a point to keep in touch with his former students from Liberia, especially those who had moved to America. I visited him frequently, gathering whatever news I had recently obtained about the state of Liberia to make conclusions about where my family could be. Roy had a thick gray mustache and beard that accented his pink face and head, a beard that shriveled as he spoke with an unlikely Liberian accent.

I entered Roy's office and immediately headed to a chair between overflowing boxes. Stacks of papers were piled on and around his desk and the tables around the office. He was writing something, but stood up as soon as I walked in to give me a hug.

"Here's the new mom," he said in that way he spoke to his Liberian friends, words singing. He looked at me like many people did that year—he was sorry for me and covered it with a smile.

"I trying," I said, sitting down. I didn't remove my coat, still mistrusting New York winters.

"Are you sure you had baby?" Roy asked.

"Thank you," I said.

"How is the boy? You're eating?"

"Everybody's doing well," I said. "Facia's been helping."

"That's good."

"And yes, I'm eating. I'm taking care of myself for the baby," I continued.

"Good. You hear anything yet?"

"Not after Amos's call," I said. "That why I'm here, actually."

Roy listened carefully, as he always did.

"I decided I'm going back," I said.

The chair Roy sat in swiveled and he creased his eyebrows.

"I've been praying about it and it is the only option since the people still fighting. I have to go get them," I continued.

"Mam," he interrupted, "I assume I am not the first person who's said this and I won't be the last, but this is very risky."

"I know."

"Very risky."

"It's my only option. I can't concentrate on anything knowing they still in hiding. Who knows when the fighting will stop?"

"Still, it's very risky," Roy said. "You don't want to wait? They say it will be over soon."

"They said that before it started and now look," I argued. "Facia has a friend in Sierra Leone I can stay with while I try to cross the border and get to Lai."

"Mam, that isn't possible," he said.

"Some months ago I didn't know where they were. I thought they were dead," I said. "I have this information and I have to do something with it."

"Okay. Okay," Roy said. "How? Tell me how you plan to go about this."

I had thought about it for weeks. I had rehearsed their escape day and night while I fed and held my new son, his face so familiar, so much like Gus's. I thought of it in every class, distracted during lectures about the details.

"I want to leave in one month's time. Early December. I will go to

Sierra Leone to Facia's friend in Freetown. I hear I can take a bus to the border town and rent a room, and Facia says once I am there I can find people who can send word to them in the village that I am close. Lai is close to that border town. Only one day walking. That way Gus can come meet me there and I can bring them back," she said.

"But what if you don't find someone who is willing to go? Few people will risk their lives to go back into Liberia," he said.

"Then I will try to sneak in and get them out," I continued.

"They are not letting people in like that-oh," he said.

"I would find a way."

"But—"

"Roy," I said, my voice almost breaking, "I have already made up my mind. I am not here to—I just need to know how many weeks of class I can miss before I lose my scholarship. And . . . and I need to know how to get a sponsorship letter to present to the embassy in Freetown, so I can bring them here on my student visa."

Roy turned back toward his desk and rubbed his eyes.

"Please," I said.

I looked away from him at the papers around his room. I was happy to have friends who cared—I had the same conversations with Facia and friends.

"How long do you plan on staying, Mam?" Roy asked.

"Until I find them," I said. "I just want to know how long until I lose the scholarship."

"It will depend on the professor, generally, but my guess is you will have about two to three weeks into the semester before it really affects you. So the middle of February."

"So I have two months," I confirmed.

Roy nodded, reluctantly.

"And if you find them—"

"—when"

"When you find them," he edited himself, "how will you get them to New York?"

"Well, I will bring them here on my student visa," she said. "I spoke to a friend's lawyer. I just need a sponsorship letter and they will come on my student visa. I know it will take some time to get that settled with the embassy, a few weeks, but there's a crisis so I think they are expediting some cases."

"Few cases."

"I have faith. We'll be in the few," I said.

"And you have money for this?"

"I am using some of my stipend and I've been borrowing money from friends and family," I admitted. "But not much."

"I know you have made up your mind. I know you love them and I can't imagine how you feel knowing your family is stuck there," Roy said. "But I just think the best thing you can do for yourself and for them is to stay here. Gus is safe with the girls in Lai. That much you know."

"Not absolutely," I said. "But yes—Amos said he was with them until the checkpoints to Junde."

"So wait until the war is over and they return to Caldwell. Then you can think about how to bring them here with you."

"No," I said, without hesitation.

"No?"

"No," I said, folding my hands in my lap. "He would do it for me if he was in my place."

"But he is not. And he would want you to stay here," Roy continued, unwavering.

So I asked him if he had ever been close to death. Consumed by it. I asked if he ever had mornings when even waking up seemed the most unfair burden. Eating. Bathing. And even after somehow building up the courage to wake up, every thought not directly linked to them was a betrayal. The restlessness made a home on my shoulders, tormenting me as the day went on. This was the other side of love. Love gone is painful, and I existed in that grief upon hearing news of the Ol' Pa. But love almost gone—the lurking threat of loss—that was a daily torture, death realized every morning. And I did not know which was worse—the fear of losing them to the war, the fear that some rebels would find Lai and kill them before the war ended, and knowing that if such a thing did occur, I would not be able to go on; or admitting that I had already died, so many times that year, with my Ol' Pa, with Liberia and hopes of returning and making the life that we planned for, with my rosebush in Caldwell likely incinerated, with my fears that my daughters were gone, those fears that delivered the most cruel lullabies every night I did not hear from them. Such is the danger of deep love, however beautiful. Dying lingers close behind.

"And if you love someone that much, that fully, what would you do?" I asked Roy, tears raining onto the scarf wrapped around my neck.

"I would go," he said.

TWENTY-SIX

December 1990, and Freetown looked beautiful from heaven. The winding roads made a bed among Sierra Leone's hills, so green and perfect my lungs filled with clean air. I could see the palm trees from the sky, home to coconuts and unripe plantains, nuts that would make oil for some Ol' Ma's cassava leaves that night. There were many people who tried to convince me to stay before I boarded the plane at LaGuardia—but in the end their memory was the only approval I needed.

I only had one small suitcase, which I carried with me on my flight, full of those dresses I had once loved. Facia had advised me to wear my long hair in a ponytail, to try to look as though I had never left. She had reminded me that for months the women there did not have those simple things that contributed to the natural beauty of West African women—a brush, lipstick, perfume, a clean dress—so I should pack the most plain dresses possible so I would not stand out.

"They will steal from you if they know you coming from America," Facia had cautioned, taking the dresses I had packed out of my suitcase and replacing them with more plain, nondescript ones.

Before leaving our apartment, I held my son for what felt like an entire day. I nursed him, I sang to him and told him those stories my

Ol' Ma told me, and her Ol' Ma had told her. I doted on his eyes and cheeks—I promised him I would be back with his father and sisters. I was able to obtain a sponsorship letter from the scholarship program, which I would use to get visas from the American embassy for them to come to New York with me. I had tried to obtain letters for my mother and sisters, but in the end, only my immediate family would be allowed back into America with me. Since the stipend was not enough for all of their plane tickets, I asked everyone I considered a friend for help. I was able to raise enough for our tickets and had a thousand dollars left for an anticipated two-month stay.

I met with Yasuka days before my flight, and like others, Yasuka asked me if I was afraid to go, if there were other options, if I had considered and planned for the worst.

"I am not afraid, no," I answered. "I actually feel like myself again. I feel like I can breathe again."

Yasuka looked down at the table toward the barely touched cups of tea for most of the conversation. I lifted her hand and placed it on mine, which was warmer than the temperatures outside would suggest.

"I can't wait to meet them," Yasuka said, finally, gracefully shielding her fear with hopefulness, just like everyone else I told.

When I exited the plane in Freetown, I was greeted by a familiar West African warmth and stuffiness. I swore I smelled all that was mingling in a smoke pot in the distance, all those things I had missed the past year. There were two lines: one for Sierra Leoneans and one for foreigners. I went to the line for foreigners and waited amid a crowded lot of British military personnel and members of various nongovernmental organizations, all wide-eyed and noticeably overwhelmed with excitement that they, too, had arrived in Africa. The airport was loud, too loud to hear myself worry. Beyond the customs counters I noticed local men in safety vests wave toward arriving passengers, offering their help with checked luggage. I approached the front of the line. I nervously pulled out my passport from a folder of traveling papers I was keeping in a purse close to my chest. I handed it to the attendant.

"Hello," he said, examining at my passport. "Where is your address here?"

I cleared my throat and handed him a sheet of paper with the address of Facia's friend written on it.

"I am staying with Marta Raman," I said.

The man nodded and stamped my passport, letting me pass. Beyond the counter, two security guards waited for me, blocking my way to the airport exit.

"We just need to check your bag," one said.

I handed them my suitcase and watched carefully as they opened it and lifted a few of my clothes.

"Open your purse," one of them said.

I held out my purse and opened it for the guard to look inside.

"Okay, you can go," he said and pushed my valise aside. A man approached with a customs vest and paced in front of me.

"Where you coming from? London or America?" he asked.

My exit was so close. I glanced at the door.

"America, but I don't need your help," I said, remembering Facia's stories about rogues who waited at the airport for naive travelers to steal from.

"Your people outside?" he asked and I nodded.

"Let me take your bag for you," he said, gesturing toward my suitcase. "Too heavy for the beautiful lady."

"No, no," I said holding my bag close.

"Okay, okay," he said, friendly and respectfully. "I am only trying to help. Welcome, sister," he said and walked away.

I felt sorry for how short I had been with him, but the feeling was fleeting, eclipsed by my new anxiety that I had actually made it back. Outside, the sun ran to meet me, kissing my face like the sister, the child it recognized me to be. A plane flew above us out of Sierra Leone and cars honked their way out of the parking lot in jagged lines.

A man approached me wearing a newly pressed shirt. He wiped the sweat from his forehead with a handkerchief and smiled my way.

"Are you Mam?" he asked. He extended his hand toward my suitcase. Again, I pulled the suitcase and purse close.

"Yes," I said softly.

"No worry, no worry. I am Marta's driver," he laughed. He looked out onto the lot and pointed toward a car about a hundred yards away. The door opened and a short woman stepped out, straightening her dress. She waved toward me and adjusted her sunglasses. I laughed and waved to the woman.

"Oh!" I said. "Thank you. Thank you," I said to the driver and handed him my suitcase. I followed him to the car where Marta waited. The impending greeting made me anxious. I knew nothing of the woman except that she was a former classmate of Facia during her time at the University of Franche-Comté in Besançon, France.

"Hello!" Marta said, giggling. "Wow, you look just like Facia!"

I hugged her and landed a soft kiss on each cheek.

"Thank you for coming," I said.

She smelled like she had rubbed peppermint oil behind her ears. I couldn't see her eyes behind her sunglasses, but I imagined they were as kind as her voice.

"You must be famished," Marta said.

The windows had been manually rolled down and all of those delightful smells raced to meet my senses.

"I am," I answered, shyly. "Thank you again for everything."

"No, please," Marta smiled. "If you are Facia's sister, then you are my sister." She rubbed my shoulder. "It is truly brave what you are doing."

"I haven't done anything yet," I said. "I want to leave tonight for the border town if possible. I could at least get there in the early morning."

"Nonsense!" Marta said, hitting the seat playfully. "You just arrived. Please. I had my house girl make you jollof rice. And we can make palaver sauce if you want. Plus, it's better to arrive in the afternoon. Especially now."

I reluctantly agreed. The driver hit the brakes hard as schoolchildren crossed the road. The Freetown intersections were swarming, more packed than I remembered from my visits when I was younger. On the other side of the street, the children danced and chased each other through the passing crowd. One turned around and made a face at us, twisting his mouth and nose in opposite directions, before continuing with his friends.

"Don't mind them," Marta laughed, noticing the child's face. "Their gut is full. Everybody happy about Christmas."

"Yes, yes." I breathed in the day's sighs. "I can't believe it's been a year since I've been back."

"Time does fly, doesn't it?" Marta asked, not missing a beat.

"There are so many people," I said.

"Yes, many of your people have come this year. Nobody ever imagined this could happen to Liberia. I remember we were all once trying to cross your borders for jobs. Now it's Liberians looking for jobs everywhere else since things do not look like they are changing."

"Wow."

"I hear Guinea and Ghana, and even Nigeria, have many more in refugee camps," Marta said.

I wondered how many of the friends were in those camps.

"They say they are setting up settlement programs in New York for those in the camps. In Staten Island, I believe," Marta said.

"Yes, I've heard that too," I said, staring at the many pedestrians on the road. "And also Rhode Island, is what they are saying."

"Yes, there too."

"This is all still unbelievable," I said.

"Yes, it's too bad," Marta said. "You know there are rumors now that Taylor's rebels are on their way through Sierra Leone. They want to overthrow Momoh too."

"We heard it but we didn't know how true it was," I said.

"I am making my way out of this place myself soon. I will go to France and wait it out."

"We will pray."

A boy approached our window selling fried plantains. I imagined he would place that day's earnings in a pot near his front door, to be used by a shy but stern mother or Ol' Ma, or a tired but joyous father or Ol' Pa. I handed him a few coins. He smiled when he saw the money and grabbed a few of the bags out of his bucket.

"No," I said waving my hand.

He nodded in gratitude as the car drove away from the intersection. I retrieved a handkerchief out of my purse and pressed it against my forehead. The heat filled the back seat as the car once again stopped in traffic.

"You will be broke in a week's time that way," Marta said laughing.

"It's a good thing I won't be here for long then," I said.

"So you were serious about leaving soon then?"

"Yes," I said. "I have to. I will leave for Bo Waterside first thing in the morning."

"Yes, well, anything we can do to help," Marta agreed. "We will take you first thing. Do you know anyone there?"

"No," I said. "I will find a room to rent and decide what to do from there."

"You really are as brave as Facia claims," Marta said. "Well, I will give you my number. You can call me just in case."

Marta's flat was the same size as my suite in New York. She lived in the middle of Freetown where the voices of laughter and soccer balls lasted through the day. The smell of burning coal stalked the bathroom from a tiny window with iron bars. The water pressure in the shower was low and the water was cold, but I stood underneath shivering. The nervousness came to me at once—the noise outside shaking my confidence, those faces on the road with no trace of my family. I had no plan beyond taking the bus to Bo Waterside and finding a room. Marta confirmed that it was nearly impossible to cross the border, but I tried to remain hopeful. Bo Waterside was so close to Junde, only a day's journey—and Lai was a canoe ride outside Junde. Surely there were people in the town who would be familiar with the area. I wrapped myself in a towel and gazed into a mirror. I had kept my hair in a ponytail as Facia had suggested, so my cheekbones were especially high below my sunken eyes. I remembered what Ol' Ma had told me about coming home if I was ever unable to recognize myself in the mirror.

"I'm here, Ma," I said.

That night, Marta's cook boiled a pot of white rice. She boiled pork meat, chicken breasts, shrimp, and smoked fish in another pot with diced onion and peppers. She took the meat out of the pot and emptied most of the salty, seasoned water. She placed jute leaves in the left-over water until it boiled, the sound like joking Ol' Pas on a dry-season porch who fought with the sun to stay a little longer behind the sugar-cane fields. The smell of the seasoned leaves filled the apartment, making my mouth water. The cook then emptied the bowl of boiled meats into the boiling greens and added palm oil, along with fresh peppers and other seasoning. Palaver sauce. When the greens were finished, she placed them over the rice she had prepared and took two plates out for me and Marta. I thanked her and stared at the bowl, its steam rising in perfect undulations. I had no appetite, bullied by nerves, but I forced myself to eat for energy.

Once when I was young, I got sick and lost my appetite for days, becoming so frail that it worried Ol' Ma and Ol' Pa. Ol' Ma made me a bowl of checked rice with okra and gravy, frying two of the best chickens on the farm in Lubn Town. She took it to the bed where I lay, next to the lantern that made a titan of her shadow.

"Eat," Ol' Ma had said, and I shook my head.

"You must eat," Ol' Ma said again, and I still refused.

"Then what will you do when the Mamy Wateh witch and the dragons them come for you? You will need energy if Pa not here to save you." That had gotten my attention, and I opened my mouth for Ol' Ma to feed me.

"And with each bite, pray for your strength against those bad bad things," Ol' Ma said, easing the metal spoon into my mouth. So with each bite at Marta's, I prayed for strength from those things, trying my best not to cry.

Early the following morning, I boarded a local bus in Freetown headed to the Sierra Leone–Liberia border town of Bo Waterside. Marta asked if I wanted to keep any of my belongings in Freetown, but I took my entire suitcase and purse with me. Inside the bus I placed the suitcase on the seat near the window and I held my purse in my lap, squeezing it against my stomach. I was told by Marta's driver to occupy my own row if I could, to avoid pickpockets who frequently used the transit for extra income. He had also said to sit at the aisle seat instead of the window, so in the unlikely event of a carjacking or other emergency, I could more easily escape. The advice had given me angst and I trembled as I boarded, and I concluded that I would pray during the entire nine-hour bus ride. There were two holes in the back windows, made by bullets. The seats on the bus were covered with old vinyl that had been tied with string or taped at bursting corners. I found an empty row in the middle and sat.

The bus passengers were mostly traders who traveled back and forth from Freetown to the border towns for goods to sell in market. The bus was less rank than I thought it would be, and I was glad that the morning breeze crept through the opened windows. As the bus pulled off, there was a loud knocking at the front door. The driver cursed while he opened the door, and a short man boarded, paying him and moving through the bus to find a seat. I looked toward the window in hopes that he would not try to sit beside me. I heard his heavy footsteps approach, and the man stopped right in front of my seat.

"Please, can I sit?" he asked.

I examined his face. His skin was the same color as his dark eyes, he was graying, and he had short fingers tightly wrapped around the handle of a duffle bag. I looked around the crowded bus and stood, picking up my suitcase, to let him slide into the window seat. The man was short—even shorter than me—and looked up at me when I stood. I placed my suitcase underneath the seat in front of me, watching it carefully as the bus continued on.

"Thank you," the man said. "I am Jallah."

I nodded but did not respond, afraid to encourage conversation, and I continued in silence as the bus rode along. The faces of pedestrians and city buildings sitting too close together became deep and vast plains. The Atlantic Ocean was not too far away, and my head leaned against its jubilant sound. Gus had courted me in the presence of that same ocean. I was a teenager when we met, and while we were undergraduates at the University of Liberia, he spent all his spare change on bus fare to visit me and my parents in Logan Town. Ol' Ma liked him because he was as brave as Ol' Pa had been, direct with his intentions, yet soft when he looked at me. The ocean had eavesdropped when he proposed.

I had been unable to sleep the night before. I lay awake in Marta's guest bed for hours anticipating my journey. Now these distant beaches ushered me to sleep, applauding my return after what felt like a lifetime away. Every time I dozed off, I woke up suddenly, surveying my surroundings with my purse close to my breasts. The suitcase remained underneath the seat.

The man laughed beside me.

"Do not worry," he said. "It is still there. I am watching it for you." I moved uncomfortably in the stiff bus seat.

"Thank you," I said quietly. I leaned my head against the seat.

"Besides, it is not thieves we must worry about. Everybody is too nervous going this way to steal," he chuckled. He looked out of the bus window and I finally smiled. His voice was warm and familiar.

"Thank you," I said again, making sure he heard me.

"Ah, no worry, no worry."

"What was your name again?" I asked after a moment. He turned to face me, noticeably pleased.

"Jallah," he said. "Yours?"

"My family calls me Mam," I answered. "I'm Vai."

"Oh! You are Vai?" he asked, holding out his hand. I shook it.

"Yes. It's nice to meet you," I said.

"I knew it," he said in Vai. "Our women are the most beautiful. That's what I say."

I laughed with him and blushed.

"*Bie-kah.* Thank you," I responded in Vai.

"You have been away, yes?"

Just as Facia had told me, my time in America was emanating from me, even with the plain clothes and hair.

"No worry, I will not hurt you. Anyway, you are clever to be so quiet, but you are safe. By my word," Jallah said, holding up his right hand. "I knew that too," Jallah said, joyfully slapping his thigh. "You should be careful traveling when you reach the border towns. I hear that not too long ago they kidnapped a woman they thought was an American nurse. They still looking for her."

I looked out the window.

"But no worry, no worry. You Vai girl and Vai people they not humbugging much, they say. You going to market?"

"No, to Bo Waterside. I need to find a room," I said.

"There are plenty rooms there but not all of them good," Jallah said. "You have family there?"

"I have family in Cape Mount," I said. "On the other side."

"Yes, me too," Jallah said. "Plenty family in Cape Mount."

"Oh, that's good."

"I have many many brothers and sisters. Many of them. Nobody die in war yet. One cousin we can't find but nobody die yet," he said.

"That's good to hear," I said, my body now cold. "What do you do?" I asked, changing the subject.

"Me, I am a trader. I go to Freetown for things you can only find in America and London and I sell and trade with the boys at the border," he said.

"That's good," I said.

"People want American things plenty. Perfume and jeans, jewelry, anything they buy if it's from America."

"That is something. People in school in America ask me where they can find African masks and fabric. They pay plenty money for it," I said.

"Yes, I know, I know. People want American thing. American want African thing," Jallah said. "Nobody just happy with what they have."

"Yeh," I agreed.

"You will see the market at Bo Waterside. American thing there too," Jallah said.

"I'm sure," I said. "But the first thing I have to do is find a room."

"I have rooms and I would let you rent one but my wives will get jealous." He laughed again until he coughed. I laughed too. I couldn't help it.

"The two of them are hard women—my wives. The people them ask why I choose them, but the heart wants what it wants," Jallah said. "How many wives did your father marry?" he asked.

"One," I said.

"Oh! And your grandfather?"

"One," I said.

"Both of them?"

"Yes."

"Wow. And still wealthy enough to have daughter in America? They are great men," Jallah said, waving his pointer finger.

"They were great women," I replied.

Jallah looked at the golden band hugging my slender finger.

"And how long have you been married?"

"Eight years. Our anniversary was last week. December 12."

"Happy anniversary," Jallah said. "You are beautiful woman. I am sure he will buy you plenty fine gifts."

I touched my ring.

"He is alive?" Jallah asked.

"Yes. I was told he is living."

"That's good! You never know, my sister," he continued in Vai. "I met a woman in Freetown who was selling at a market to feed her daughters. She said her husband and brother were killed and she cannot find her son."

"God bless her," I said.

"Yes-oh."

"And is he at Bo Waterside?" Jallah asked.

"No, he is in a village on the other side. I am going to try to get him and my daughters out," I said, each word heavier than the last.

Jallah raised his eyebrow and turned to the window. When he looked at me again, his eyebrows were still creased, unable to filter his doubtful thoughts.

"And . . . and how will you do that, sister?" he asked.

"I don't know, Jallah," I said. "Not sure yet. I hope to get answers once I reach the border."

"Ah," he said with warmth in his eyes. "You women are mighty. God bless you, sister."

He turned away from me again to face the window. I appreciated his company and goodwill. I fell asleep again and when I woke, the bus had stopped. Surprisingly, Jallah was not beside me, but outside facing the field peeing, the shortest in a line of men. I glanced down the aisle and the driver was outside stretching. My luggage was still under my seat where I left it and my purse was in my lap. After twenty minutes or so, Jallah and the others boarded the bus. I stood up to let him in.

"Sorry-oh," he said. "I did not want to wake you so I jumped over your legs. I thought sure I would disturb you but you were in a deep sleep."

"Oh yes. I am tired. I have not gotten sleep lately but it is hard to stay awake with the ocean so close. Even on a bumpy road," I said, still high with slumber. "How much longer?"

"*Nani*," he said. Four hours.

"Oh, good," I said. The noon sun made the bus even hotter than it had been that morning. I took my handkerchief from my purse and wiped the sweat from my forehead.

"You know, I was thinking," Jallah said. "I want to help you."

"Oh?" I asked.

He leaned in toward my seat and looked over his shoulder and across the aisle to see if anyone was listening. I was startled by this and I pulled away.

"No, no," he said. "Listen." He began to speak in Vai again.

"I did not want to seem too anxious before, and you can never be sure who you are talking to. But I have been thinking, I know of a woman. A rebel," Jallah said quietly. "She is a Vai woman like your-self but she grew up in the city and she joined Taylor's army." My heart beat quickly and I sunk like stone in my seat. "Don't be afraid," Jallah continued. "Listen to what I am saying. I will tell you what I learned, what everybody learns during wartime. Not all fighters are bad. They all look bad. There is blood on their clothes. They high. Most fighters, they will do bad things, but not all of them are bad. Do you understand? Some of these rebels them they get forced to fight, they have no choice, but they stay good. You understand what I saying?"

"No," I whispered, my heart still racing. I thought for a moment that perhaps Jallah was a rebel in disguise. If I screamed, the driver would stop the bus and it would lengthen my trip to Bo Waterside. And who knew if the people on the bus would turn against me if I prolonged their trip?

"Let me explain," Jallah said. "They go to villages and to some poor towns near the cities, the rebel leaders them, and they tell the young people to come join their army for money. They say, 'I will make you rich, come fight for me. I will make you commander. Make you king. Make you chief.' They promise them their family will be safe during the war and they will make money to send to them, so many of them, they say yes. Then the others who say no, they force them. They beat the boys, rape the girls them until they agree to join their army. So many still trying to be right with God even with all the bad bad things they now do, you understand?"

"What are you saying? I don't understand," I said, shaking my head.

"I know this woman, this girl her name is Satta. She is Vai and she is with Taylor army but but—" he leaned in again, so close to my ear. "If you pay her enough money, she will go and get your family for you."

"What?!" I asked loudly.

"Not too loud," Jallah said as the bus passengers looked our way. I gestured my apologies to them and looked at Jallah.

"When the rebels see her passing with people, they do not humbug her, and she learned this while saving some neighbors of hers who were Krahn," he said. "And you know what is happening to Krahn people."

"I know, I know," I said, desperately wanting him to continue.

"So she has made a business from this," Jallah said. "You pay her and you tell her where to find your family and she will go find them and walk them across checkpoints."

"And what do you get from this?" I asked.

"Mostly just a comfortable bed in paradise. But she gives me small small change for finding people for her," he laughed.

"Of course."

"Nothing is free, sister. She can bring them to you in Bo Waterside. If you want."

"Yes, yes," I said, with hope that I could finally see a shape to. "But is it safe?" I asked in English. "Is it safe?" I asked again in Vai, quieter.

"It has been so far," Jallah said.

"Can I meet people she has helped? Just to be sure?" I asked.

Jallah shook his head, waving his finger.

"They are all gone. Those who can afford her usually run far far away from this place once they get out of Liberia," he said.

So far his proposal was my only option but I did not know this man. I thought of what Gus would do and say, or Ol' Pa or Ol' Ma. But none of them were there. Fear orbited. This man could have been a killer—a rebel himself. My husband would call me foolish for entertaining the suggestion, or for even conversing with him in the way that I had during their trip. But the griots and djelis would say that perhaps this was another sign.

"I want to meet her," I said. "Please, if I can."

"Good," Jallah said, delighted by my decision.

We arrived in Bo Waterside late that afternoon. I was happy to stretch my arms and legs. I kept Jallah in sight, now my only lead in finding my husband, my girls. Bo Waterside was twice as crowded and busy as Freetown. There were some who were running down the road, some who walked with buckets of water, bundles of belongings or other goods on their glowing black heads. Market vendors shouted to pedestrians. "Plum, plum, plum, plum" or "Rice here. Rice! Rice!" or "Who want buy salt? Salt! Salt for you!" The smell of fresh fruit mingled with the fumes of rotten and deceased things. I waved my handkerchief over my nose in the heat.

"It takes some getting used to," Jallah said, walking up behind me. "You will need a hotel first, yes?" he asked.

"Yes," I said, following him.

There was a busy road that intersected with the bustling market. Jallah pointed at the intersection. Vendors waved their goods across my face as I proceeded.

"Move from here, we are fine," Jallah said, driving them away. "You look American so they will try to sell you anything."

"How?" I asked.

"We know our people," Jallah said. "We can always tell when someone has been away."

Some trucks approached and people moved out of the road. I stepped aside as the trucks sped by. A few hundred yards in the distance, along a dusty road, I vaguely made out the checkpoint. There was Liberia, so close.

"Come, come," Jallah said and continued walking.

We turned onto the street that intersected with the market and Jallah led me directly to a zinc door, painted blue, beside an alleyway with clothes hanging on either side. I was reluctant to follow and stood at the entry.

"No, please. Come," Jallah said. "It is a good one. NGO people here," he said.

I entered a foyer with tile floors, dark and redolent of dry rice and fish. A woman, very heavy and warm, entered the foyer waving.

"Allo-oh, Jallah," she said. She went to the window and lifted the flimsy blinds so that the sunlight could make its way in. She turned around and the long, skinny braids that hung from her head followed.

"Hello, sister. This is Mam, my Vai sister," Jallah said.

"Allo-sister," the woman said loudly. She held out her hand and I shook it.

"You from America? I have room for you. I have one American man stay here. He preacher. He go to Liberia, he come back next week. You very beautiful. You stay here, I have room for you."

"Okay," I said, struggling to process everything the woman had said.

"Are there many other hotels in this area?" I asked in a low tone, peering out the window in hopes that I did not offend the woman.

"This is the best one, I tell you," Jallah said.

"What wrong? This nice place, close to everything. Close to border, to market, to everything. What wrong? Plenty American people stay here. Where you from, Freetown? You from Liberia?" the woman rambled.

"Liberia, yes," I said. "Can I see the room?"

"Yes, yes, come," the woman said and opened a cabinet against the wall. There she retrieved a key and moved a curtain at the edge of the foyer.

"I will follow," I said. Jallah and the woman laughed.

"That's good. You are smart woman. Beautiful woman. I have room for you," the woman said.

I followed them down a long and narrow hallway, lit by a skylight partially obstructed by orphaned leaves and garbage on the roof. The woman opened the third door and handed me the key.

"Here your room, sister," she said and I saw clearly all of her small teeth.

The tile floors had been swept and the glass windows were barred from the outside. There was a metal bucket in the corner. The bed was made of dried mud, and cords of straw broke through a thin mattress.

"Straw mattress?" I asked.

"Yes, the very very best. Stay here. Bathroom down hall. We have running water. Your room."

I gazed at the tiny room.

"Only ten dollar one night. American dollar," the woman added.

"Okay," I said. "I'll take it."

"Good, good."

"Come, come with me outside," Jallah said. I was tired and hungry. I nodded and followed Jallah to the road outside.

"Here, take my number," he said, writing his number on a sheet of paper. "She has phone inside. She is nice woman. The building has security. You will see."

Down the dusty road, crowds continued to move throughout. I could tell those who had recently made it out of Liberia. Their clothes almost swallowed them whole and behind their eyes something had been taken.

"I will go call Satta and bring her here. Stay close by and I will call if there is trouble," Jallah said. "I must go home now but please believe me you are safe, sister."

"Okay," I said confidently. "*Bie-kah*," I said in Vai and hugged him.

Jallah disappeared into the crowd, his duffle bag dancing against his leg as he walked. I stared at the zinc door and instead of going back inside I strolled to the market road where dozens of vendors and traders were teeming, yelling above each other to ensure the last deal of the day. As I passed, women turned their heads in the direction I walked. There was one woman in particular who wore a lappa decorated with black traditional masks wrapped around her head. She was a heavyset woman who waddled as she moved intently toward me.

"You want me braid your hair?" she asked.

"No, thank you," I answered and quickened my pace to a market table I had noticed while walking with Jallah, a table with metal silverware strewn across it. I approached the vendor and those who were standing before the table parted for me.

"Allo, Ol' Ma," the vendor said.

"You want salt, Ol' Ma?" a vendor asked.

"No," I said.

"Ma, T-shirt for you. Good price," another said.

"No, no," I said, more convincing.

"One knife and fork please," I said with authority. The silverware clanged and screeched as the man found a pair for me.

"Butter good for you?" he asked.

"Steak," I said. "Please."

"Just one set?" he asked, and the others around the table glanced at me askance.

"No, a set of four," I corrected myself.

"That will be one dollar American," the man said and wrapped the metal in a sheet of newspaper. I paid him, and grabbing my purchase, I rushed to the next vendor, a woman selling *kala*.

"*Kala, kala, kala,* fresh *kala* bread," the woman said.

"Yes, two bags please," I said.

"For you one dollar American. Usually two dollar but I give it to my sister," the woman said.

I paid her and put the bread in my purse.

Back at the hotel, the woman was sitting in the foyer against her locked cabinet.

"Allo-oh!" she said when she saw me. "There now, I tell you I'm the best one."

I quickly paid the woman and went to my room, locking the door behind me. I sat on the bed and listened closely for threatening noises—signs to confirm that I was moving in the right direction—but nothing could be heard above my beating heart.

That night, I unfolded the silverware from its wrapping. I gripped the handle of a steak knife and took it to bed with me. The straw from the mattress poked at me from every angle. I closed my eyes but I knew I would not sleep well. The darkness was deep except for a dribble of moonlight that entered my window in streams. I held the knife close to me, waiting in the night, unsure of whether or not I slept.

TWENTY-SEVEN

Jallah did not show up the next day. When he still did not come on the following day, I began to call the number he had given me every hour of the following day, and the day after that, beginning at dawn.

"No worry, he come," the proprietor had said, recognizing the number in my hand every time I emerged from the room to use the telephone. "He good man. He come back."

During my second afternoon, I used the phone to call Facia to tell her all that had happened and to ask advice, but the service was so poor that I could tell by Facia's response that she wasn't hearing all that she was being told.

"You are well? You made it to Bo Waterside?" Facia asked several times.

"Yes, I am well," I yelled. "I am here."

"Service to America not good this time. Wait for night, you try again," the boarder said. I did not know Marta well enough to call her, and I did not want to worry her with trouble so soon.

I waited in my room for most of the day and slept with my knife by my side during the night. I heard other boarders in neighboring rooms, their snores loud. I brought a book with me but was too distracted to read. I looked over the papers in my purse, including the letter from my Fulbright sponsor that I would present to the American embassy in Freetown. I pressed my fingers against the letters, along the lines of each of my daughters' names, my tears staining the page. I frequently took out all of the dresses from my valise and shook them for bugs, then folded them again and neatly placed them in my bag. I sat facing the wall, then stood against the door facing the window. On a few evenings I went outside and strolled up and down the street and around the market, listening for any news of what was happening on the other side. I would always hurry back, afraid I would miss the call. It had been almost one week and I resolved that if Jallah did not return by the end of the week, I would attempt to cross the border myself. I decided this while pacing my room, my slippers beating the tile floor.

"Come," I heard the boarder yell outside. "Mam, sister come!"

I ran out of my room to the foyer, where the boarder had placed the phone on the counter.

"That him," she said and smiled. "See, I tell you."

"Hello? Jallah?" I asked, my nerves fluttering.

"Yes, I found the girl," he said cheerfully.

"Good! I have been trying to call you!"

"Yes, I was trying to find her. We will come to you tomorrow morning. No worry," he said. He had hung up the phone quickly, and I stood in the void with his tarrying words.

"Good, right?" the boarder asked, gathering her braids into a ponytail above her neck. I nodded.

"All good," I said.

On the following morning I kneeled before my bed, resting my knees on the hem of my dress, and I prayed, murmured my thanksgiving before asking God for favor. The boarder let me borrow two folding chairs for Jallah and the woman to sit.

"Can't we meet in the foyer?" I had asked.

"You can," the boarder said in a low tone, lower than I had ever heard her speak. She then came close to me. "But some meetings should be private."

"Yes," I said. "I understand."

Jallah and Satta arrived an hour later and the boarder knocked on my door. I stood up from my bed, where I had hidden the knives at either end of the straw mattress.

Jallah shook my hand and gestured toward the girl behind him.

"This is her. Satta," he said.

Satta was wearing camouflage pants and a stained shirt. Her short hair was braided into cornrows with endings that jutted out from behind her ears. She had stocky shoulders for her small frame, and her eyes were red and sunken, fighting to be desirous again. She nodded toward me and took a seat on one of the chairs against the wall. I sat on the mattress.

"So, uh, as I told you, Satta, our Vai sister has family still in Liberia," Jallah said, trying to ease us, but he sounded so unnatural that it worried me.

"You are Vai?" I asked Satta, in Vai.

"Yes," Satta answered in English. "Where is your family?"

I looked at Jallah. He waved at me to speak, assuring me that the woman was trustworthy.

"They are hiding in a village near Junde," I said. "You are Vai. Was your family's village close to there?"

"I know the area," Satta said shortly. "Yeh."

"Yeh, it is longer to get there by foot. You have to go through the forest. The easiest way is by canoe," I said.

"Yes, I know."

"From Junde," I said. I tried to speak to Satta in Vai again but I sensed that the woman did not want to talk about anything personal.

"Jallah said you have done this before? You ever had trouble?" I asked.

"No. Never trouble. Me, I just wear my full suit and carry my gun," she said pointing to her back. "They don't humbug me. They think I transporting."

"A gun? You ever had to use it?" I asked.

"Not when I working like this, no," Satta said and looked away from my face.

"And what is transporting?"

"Taking civilians someplace. To rebel leader, to town, holding them for questioning, anything," she said. Beneath the toll the war had taken, as Satta spoke, I thought that she was beautiful, her skin and eyes once youthful and forgiving. I wondered what had made her this way, what had undone all that was remarkable about this woman.

"I do this plenty. No worry," Satta said. "I help your family. Me, my family gone. I go bring your family, trust me, Ol' Ma." She looked at me. I became more hopeful.

"I don't want to offend you, but how do I know you will not harm them? That you will not leave them somewhere?"

"How I know you na spy?" Satta asked. "Somebody working for my boss in pretty dress so I confess and you tell them to kill me."

Her smile tiptoed onto her face but it arrived. And it was the smile and the childhood I saw underneath, stolen but still emerging at moments I least expected it, that made up my mind.

"How long will it take?" I asked. "How long will it take to get to Lai?"

"One day."

"One day?! You know where that is?"

"Yes, we will walk, then take bus at Junde. No worry," Satta said.

"That is so soon," I said and could not hold in the tears. I wiped them quickly, afraid to seem weak before the rebel. "One day?"

"Aye, sister, no worry," Jallah said, clapping his hands together. "Satta do this plenty."

At Columbia my concentration was history. I examined Satta and remembered all those women I had read about—Helen of Troy, Cleopatra—and thought of all the times I had wondered which woman would be that for Liberia. This once nameless woman—Satta— Liberia's unlikely heroine and her sisters, existed. I wiped my eyes again.

"How much?" I asked.

"How many people?"

"My husband and my daughters. Three daughters. Four of them in total."

"How old your daughters?" Satta asked.

"They are babies. Four, five, and the oldest just turned seven in November."

"Okay," Satta said. "Six hundred American. Three hundred for the man and one hundred each for children."

The price was higher than I expected, and what I knew was a risky choice. But. It was my only choice. Satta and Jallah waited in the silence as I deliberated to myself.

"I will go for you. I will bring them back to you. You will see," Satta said.

"When . . . when would you leave?"

"I leave later today. I travel in the night and get there tomorrow morning. They will be here by tomorrow evening time."

"Yes, she will bring them to my house," Jallah said. "You can leave here and come wait there with me until they come. I spoke to my wives about them. Then you all take the bus the next morning back to Freetown."

I did not need any more convincing. I grew more and more excited as they plotted. I imagined kissing my daughters' faces again.

"Okay. I will do it," I said. "Please leave soon."

I asked Jallah and Satta to wait outside in the foyer while I put the money into a sheet of newspaper. I gathered my things to leave with Jallah, to wait at his home while Satta went to Lai. I gave Satta the package of money and Satta placed it into her deep pockets. She held out her hand and I shook it, then hugged her. Satta flitted uncomfortably in the embrace.

"Thank you," I said. "Thank you so much."

"You go now?" the boarder yelled down the hallway and hurried into the foyer. "You come back then!" She shook my hand and patted Jallah on his shoulder.

Outside, the sun, heat, and border sounds charged toward us. Satta headed in a different direction than Jallah and I did. Those who were on the road avoided eye contact with her, some quickening their pace when they noticed the young rebel.

"Where are you going?" I yelled.

"You want to see them, yeh?" Satta replied, before pressing on. I nodded and continued on with Jallah.

"No worry," Jallah said. "She come with your family."

"Wait!" I said, turning around, calling after Satta. I reached into my purse and retrieved a five-by-seven photograph.

"What?" Satta asked when I reached her.

"Take this. Show it to him," I said. "He will not go unless you show him that picture."

"Okay, okay," Satta said and folded the photograph, stuffing it into her pocket.

"Tomorrow evening," Satta said, leaving us again.

"Tomorrow evening," I said. I could hear the birds again. The smell of frying food awakened me, and amid those passing by, I heard music, and hummed along to it as Satta disappeared.

DRY
SEASON

TWENTY-EIGHT

"I come for you," Satta said, spitting on the ground in front of Papa. "You and your daughters."

"What do you mean you come for me?" he asked, raising his voice. "Who sent you?" Her gun was the same as those carried by the rebels on the road.

"Mam. Your wife," she answered and watched Papa's face transform into muddled disbelief and confusion. He stood noiselessly. "Your wife come for you."

"Nonsense. Leave from here. We have no money for you."

"I did not come for money," she said. "Here, look. I buy food for you." Satta pushed forward the jug of palm oil and laid the bag of rice over her shoulder on the ground. She opened up the large bag and pulled out a bag of rice, greens, and other meat she had purchased from the market. Papa was wide-eyed when he saw the food. He shook his head at the bag, not fully trusting Satta. He had seen too many in her uniform killing.

"She say to bring you food. She here now," Satta said.

"Leave here. These people don't want trouble."

Papa looked down at us.

"I said go in the house! Go to Ol' Ma and close the door!" he yelled at us.

Too stunned to leave him, we instead hid behind his legs. Several villagers came to Papa's aid as he argued with the woman. He tried to convince her to leave and she became frustrated trying to convince him that it was Mam who sent her.

It had been one year since we saw her, and the more the woman spoke, the more I wanted to just go with her to see what was on the other side of those words.

"What's wrong?" Ol' Ma said, reaching us in the middle of the village circle. She looked down at the food.

"Ma, please take the girls," Papa said.

"What she want?" Ma asked.

"Ol' Ma, if this man is Augustus, his wife say I come get him and take him and his daughters to meet her."

"Where?!" Ma shouted.

"Ma, don't listen," Papa said. "Please leave."

"She is in Bo Waterside. She say to come get her husband and three daughters," Satta said.

Ol' Ma glanced at Papa.

"Of course, they standing right here," Papa said skeptically. I saw sweat on his head and I felt it against his clothes. "Listen, I don't know how you know my name or how you knew we were here but I don't want trouble."

"Wait, wait," Satta said. "She said show you this. This picture."

She took the photograph out of her pants pocket, unfolded it, and handed it to Papa.

His body shook in my grasp and he shouted. He could have fallen to the ground in the circle if we were not surrounding him. He shouted again and laughed, in that yawning, beautiful way that laughter comes after it has been resting for too long.

"What's there?" Ol' Ma asked.

He held out the photograph to Ma. It was Mam sitting on a couch beside a baby that she had propped up with a pillow. On the back she had written: Gus, my love. Here is your son. Augustus Moore Jr. Born October 7, 1990.

"I have a son," Papa said, barely audible. "I have a son!" he yelled, waving the photo. My sisters and I jumped and reached for his hand to view the picture, screaming and clapping at the little human, and our Mam, who sat smiling beside him. Ol' Ma placed her hand over her mouth and started dancing.

The villagers ran out to the commotion. They passed around the picture, pointing at it and patting Papa on the back. I knew that it all meant that I would see Mam again. Maybe I would even see her America and find out why she had been away for so long, why she had not been in Caldwell to shield our heads when the bullets fell.

The clapping and the stomping of their feet made a rhythm we all danced to. She said that Mam was here. She said that I had a brother.

"When will we see Mam?" I asked, looking up at Papa, jumping.

"Yes, please," Satta said. "I tell her I take you back this evening. We must leave now."

"Now?" Papa asked.

"The only way we go back by sundown," Satta said.

"Not much time."

"Yes, we go through Junde walking and take bus some of the way. Long way so we leave after you eat," she said.

"Where is she?" Papa asked.

"Bo Waterside. She stay there and wait for you," Satta said.

"How long she been here?" my aunty asked among the crowd.

"I don't know. I only come to take her people to her," Satta said. "But we go today. She take you to Freetown."

"So you going to America!" a villager shouted and they continued to rejoice, given hope by our salvation.

When Papa finally agreed, food was prepared on the smoke pot in the cookhouse and we were fed rice with gravy and chicken. We were then taken back to Ol' Ma's house, where she gathered the few dresses we still had and put them in a plastic bag.

"Ol' Ma, you come too?" I asked her.

She sat on her bed and extended her hands for us to come to her. Her tears washed our faces, her kiss so familiar.

"No, I stay here," she said finally. "But you be a good girl for your father."

Our excitement was now corrupted by the news that we were leaving Ol' Ma behind, and we cried.

"But you come too?" we asked again.

"No, but we see each other again soon. You go to America and become big girl and come back to see me. When all of this over. You send for me."

Anger triumphed over my other emotions, then sadness and regret. Who would be my listener now? And who would lie beside her on the nights she cried for Ol' Pa, wishing I was big enough to protect her, as she had so graciously protected me.

"I see you soon," she said, wiping her face with the colors of her lappa. "Look, you must smile when you see Mam. She want see you happy. She'n see you for long, and you must smile for her," she said in Vai. "Show me the smile you will show her."

Ol' Ma stood up from the bed and held my shoulders.

"Show me," she said again.

I thought of Mam, and of the baby in the picture, and of America. It was hard to do, but I wanted to make Ol' Ma happy. So I smiled.

"There it is!" she said.

I was relieved by the sound of her voice, her haunting face. I crashed into her, hands squeezing her waist. She hugged my sisters and me, fighting her tears, and pulled us away.

"You must go to Mam. Go and you all make Ol' Ma proud-yeh?" she said.

A neighbor stood in the doorway.

"They waiting, Ol' Ma," he said.

"Okay, we come," Ol' Ma said.

Papa waited in the village circle with Satta. We took turns hugging friends and family, each goodbye making me heavier and heavier, so that when we turned around to leave, K on Papa's shoulders and

Wi and me each holding a hand, my steps were painful. My footprints were deep and the sand crept through the holes of my slippers. I turned around at the waving collective as we approached the canoe. There had been so many goodbyes, but none had felt like this. That waving crowd of protectors, watchers of my childhood. Papa squeezed my hand. He lifted each of us from the sandy shore, placing us carefully in the teetering canoe.

"We going to see Mam?" I asked Papa again through the stuttering tears. Satta sat across from us in the canoe, her gun tall behind her back.

"Yes," Papa said, this time without hesitation.

I leaned against him, looking back once more at those on the shore, my Ol' Ma in front of the crowd. I wanted to touch the lake. I wanted to put some of Lake Piso's water in my mouth and rinse out the bitter taste.

TWENTY-NINE

We walked with Satta until the sun almost left the sky, toward a town called Vonzuan, north of Junde. I was finally full from the food Satta had brought, after seven months of surviving off the baby fish that the fishers were able to catch, but I was tired from crying for Ol' Ma and kept tugging at Papa's shirt to get him to hold me. Those walking on the road scurried away when they saw Satta, her gun hitting her leg with every step. Papa followed close behind her.

I looked up at Satta's bare, dark neck below her stunted braids. She was not like Mam or my aunties or the other women in the village. She did not walk like them, but she did not walk like Papa either. She did not walk like the rebels on the road. She was different. When other big people moved in the war, they were not certain about their next steps. They did not know if they would remain on the road or have to run into a swamp to dodge rockets or tanks. But Satta knew the steps she would take. She was smaller than other big people, shorter though her shoulders were wide, but she walked in a bigger way than them, godlike with the certainty of her steps. When we crossed the paths of other rebels, I felt Papa's reluctance. He walked slower as he followed Satta, pulling us close to his leg. She would nod at the rebels or stop and talk, though only for a short while, and we waited with Papa close by. Some of them yelled at Satta and looked at us for a moment before letting her pass. But most looked at her for a long time, up and down and up and down, like Papa looked at Mam. I wondered if Satta had met Hawa Undu and if she had tried to talk him out of this war. If he had looked at her this way too. The farther we walked, the more crowded the road became.

"We going to see Mam?" I asked.

"Yes. We see her soon," Papa said.

Sometimes while we were walking I felt his leg shake. He was sweating and his breathing was faster than the times we were walking after leaving Caldwell. I was so tired that I eventually stopped.

"Come. Come, we have to keep going," Papa said.

"No, I tired."

"What wrong with the girl?" Satta asked, turning around. "Let's keep going-oh," she said standing close to Papa.

"Tutu, we have to go. Let's go see Mam," he said, tugging at my hand. With each step, my feet were reacquainted with a merciless pang. Papa leaned forward, still holding K, and kissed my head.

"We will be home soon, yeh? Tell me . . . say to me the memory verse you just learned. You remember, yeh?"

"I remember," Wi said behind him.

"Good. Good girl, Wi," Papa said and leaned down and kissed her head. "Say it for me. Say it with your sister."

"The Lord . . . the Lord is my strength and my refuge; whom shall I fear?" she said.

"Say it again, yeh?" Papa said.

"The Lord is my strength and my refuge; whom shall I fear?"

After several repetitions my crying ceased. I joined my sister's litany until my legs became numb, until those walking on the road became gray as the sun hid its face behind dormant clouds.

We made it to Vonzuan in the afternoon. We had stopped only once, to share an orange, before we were told we had to continue. There were few civilians like us in sight, and there was a junction where two mammoth tanks and other rebel cars had gathered. The tanks were deliberate in their pointing, and the boys who crowded around them were saying what I knew were bad words while they yelled and laughed together. Some were dressed like Satta. Others were not wearing T-shirts—only pants.

"Stay close," Papa said.

Satta talked to the boys, and while we waited I remembered that I would see Mam soon. I wondered if she smelled the same and if her hair would feel just as soft and cold through my fingers. Mothers do not forget their daughters, Korkor had once told me, so I knew she would recognize me, even though it had been so long since she had seen me. I wondered if she was wearing one of her colorful dresses or the lipstick that made her lips the color of plums.

Satta finally returned to where we stood. As she walked away from the boys, they whistled at her.

"They say the bus going in ten minutes. Ten minutes it will be here," she said.

"What bus?"

"To the border."

"Rebel bus we taking?" Papa asked, alarmed.

"That the only way. They letting women and children who make it to the border cross, but they hold men. They think men carry information outside."

"What?"

"That the border. No man go out. So we go with rebel transport and I get you to the other side."

The terror was clear on Papa's face. He held K's legs against his chest, her hands firm on his head as she sat on his shoulders. He looked down at me and Wi, then out toward the group of rebels several times.

"And my girls. They will be safe?"

"Yes, trust me. You with me. All will be well. They will not talk to you. They think you family," she said in a low tone.

"Okay," Papa said, finally.

Ten minutes later, a vandalized bus with writing on its body, muddy tires, and no windows pulled up to the intersection. An arm hung out of a back window and was beating the bus like a drum in a foreign, bluffing rhythm. There were a few women on the bus, and they all looked like they were around Satta's age. When the bus stopped, some of the rebel boys got out to pee in the nearby field. Ol' Ma had taught us how to close our eyes when this happened, making us promise to count to ten before opening them again. Several of the rebels at the junction gathered at the bus door to board. The ones who held weapons took them off their shoulders by the handles before boarding.

Satta waited until there were no others left to board and she tapped Papa's arm.

"Stay close," he said again, and we followed as he drew near the bus door, his pace snaillike. When we entered the bus, Satta pointed to a row in the front and Papa quickly pushed us into the seat before sitting next to the aisle. It smelled like a bathroom inside and the smoke from lit cigarettes throughout the bus filled the air around our seat. I tried turning around to see who was on the bus but Papa pinched me. He leaned down and whispered, "Look forward. Never look back. We will be there soon."

I obeyed him and kept my eyes on the road. The bus began its route and while we drove, the boys were loud behind us, using those words their Ol' Mas would have popped their mouths for saying. Satta sat across the aisle in a seat with another girl, both of their guns laid across their laps and jutting out of the bus window. Some boys in the back of the bus kept looking at Papa, and Satta went to the back to talk to them. I heard them ask her about Papa, and I think he heard it, too, because he sat with his back straight, as if he was not afraid, as if his leg was not shaking beside us.

Outside the front windows, those who were walking scattered into the fields when they noticed the bus. Papa's leg shook every time he saw this. Our rainy season escape was not so long ago that he had forgotten when we were the ones running. Papa periodically looked across the aisle at Satta and avoided turning around for fear of engaging the young rebels. There were other rebels on the road, stopping pedestrians, interrogating pedestrians, even those with children. I looked ahead until I became sleepy, and I leaned my head against Papa's shoulder to rest.

"We see Mam soon," he whispered again, though I was not sure if he was saying it for us or for himself.

The boys in the back of the bus were loud and their words, rough and mannish, bounced around the bus. There were clicking sounds as if they were playing with their guns; there was laughter, too dry to believe; and every time it became a little quiet, unrestrained laughter or more unconvincing laughter ensued.

Wi sat beside me near the window, and K was between Papa and me. He looked down at us frequently. And when he was not looking at us, eyes overcome with a worry I was not used to seeing in him, he was looking out at the road, his lips slightly moving with words too low to hear. His feet tapped the bus floor, swathed with large irremovable stains of spit.

When the bus slowed down, Papa looked across the seat at Satta, and I knew that we were even closer to seeing Mam. Almost immediately after it stopped, Papa instructed us to stand, grabbing each of our arms to exit the bus behind Satta. Outside, the rebels piled out of the bus. Some went to the road to pee while others loitered around it. Satta said goodbye to her friend and led us away from the bus. A small group of mostly women, children, and elders formed a slow-moving line that inched its way toward a massive checkpoint some fifty yards away. Their frayed lappas hung from their hips, their eyes darkened. Children were tied on some of their backs and the women periodically stepped out of the queue to catch a view, however distant and blurry, to Sierra Leone. There were many Liberian flags ahead, unmoving as they hung on poles in the stiff wind, and defaced on the sides of parked cars. Some in the line were crying, and there was chatter throughout that they were now keeping all men in holding centers, for fear that they were carrying news to opposition on the other side.

Taylor's men were manning the checkpoint and Satta scanned the faces ahead for whom she would approach with Papa. They were dressed like her and also carrying guns. Members of the rebel army stood behind tables interviewing all those who passed into Sierra Leone. It was rumored to be the most dangerous checkpoint. None were turned away. They were either allowed to pass, apprehended and held for days in rebel centers for questioning, or killed. So rather than risking the latter, many remained in hiding.

As we approached the checkpoint, Satta turned around and faced Papa.

"I will walk you close to front of line," she said. "Then I will go talk to them and tell them you with me. You must show them your identification and they will write laissez passer to Sierra Leone."

"Wait, I still have to go through checkpoint?" Papa asked.

"Yes, but no worry," Satta said. "No worry. It's for your travel pass. I talk to them. You don't have trouble."

"But my girls," he said. "If anything . . . just in case. You will—"

"—yes I take them to your wife," Satta interrupted him. "But no worry, nothing happen. We must hurry. I talk to them."

Papa nodded and Satta led us to a place in the line as promised. We strolled with the others while ahead the rebels interrogated those escaping, asking the same questions we had heard during our rainy season escape. Before we arrived at the front of the line, Papa stood us side by side and kissed each of us. He looked into our faces, his pupils widened, and beads of sweat straddled the hairs on his face.

"Papa loves you," he said. "You know that, yeh?"

"Yeh," we answered together.

Papa met the rebels at the front of the line with grace. He was calm and quiet, and we hid behind him.

"Your children?" one of them asked.

"Yeh," Papa answered.

"Tell them come from behind you."

Papa pulled our arms and we stood side by side, facing the men on the other side. They were bigger than Papa and smelled like the boys on the bus. Not too far away from them, other rebels lingered.

"Where your ID?" the rebel demanded. Papa took out his university identification from his wallet and handed it to the man.

"Let me see your bag," another said. Papa handed him the backpack he was carrying and the man opened it, sifting through our change of clothes, the documents, and Bible therein.

"Birth certificate for the girls them?" the rebel asked.

"In the bag," Papa said pointing to the bag. The man searching it threw it back at him and he rummaged through the contents for our papers.

The rebel looked at us closely and endlessly. Papa studied the bodies of those beyond the checkpoint for Satta. His hands trembled along the ragged handles of his bag. The watchfulness of the rebels burdened him, I could tell, but Papa had never let me down before. The months had withered his spirit, but he was still a giant, our giant, with hands strong enough to armor my ears when the drums echoed loudly in the night.

The man behind the table waved toward a group standing nearby on his right and another rebel approached, holding a clipboard. The man handed Papa his bag and the rebel gestured to us to follow him. Papa took our hands and we shuffled behind him. The rebel turned to Papa, his eyes cutting and frigid.

"What you do here?" the official asked.

"I am meeting my wife here," Papa replied.

"Where she?"

"She here," Papa said. "In Bo Waterside."

"Yeh, what you do here?"

"I am professor. Teacher," Papa said.

"You teacher?"

"Yeh."

He looked as though he did not believe Papa.

"Let me see your ID."

Papa again revealed his identification.

"Give me the girl papers," the official said.

Papa gave him our birth certificates from the bag. The man reviewed the documents and wrote something on his clipboard, each written word sounding like knives slicing stone. He then took a circular wooden knob out of his pocket and pressed it against the clipboard. When he was finished, he handed the papers to Papa, along with what he had written.

"Here," the official said. "Your stamp laissez passer."

He handed Papa the flimsy sheet of paper and nodded toward Satta, who stood on the side of the road, not too far from the checkpoint, waiting.

"Thank you," Papa said and we rushed to Satta.

"Come, follow me," she said as soon as we reached her, declining to show any emotion toward us in that company.

"Thank you," Papa said to Satta, under his breath as we hurried past the checkpoint. She did not turn to face him, but she nodded, her eyes fastened on the road.

And there, alongside Satta, we passed the Sierra Leonean border. Papa exhaled after we crossed that invisible line, and I felt his relief as the grip on my hand loosened, little by little with each step. For twenty minutes after passing the checkpoint and border, Satta led us to the outskirts of Bo Waterside's bustling market, where a wooden house sat on the crown of a hill. The sun was almost gone, yet the sky remained blue into the early evening. Untended fields with overgrown grass were on either side of the narrow road to the house. There was a water well in the front yard, not far from the porch. Its bucket sat on the rim and a sturdy rope was tied to the handle, suspending into the abyss below.

"She is inside there," Satta said. "My job is done."

"Wait, you are not coming?" Papa asked.

"No, this what I was paid to do. I must go now. I been gone long and other things to do tonight."

"But what if they'n there?"

"They there, no worry."

"It's just up the hill," Papa protested.

"So you go alone then. I finish," Satta said. "Go now. She wait for you."

Papa looked toward the house. He knew that he would not be able to convince Satta to continue with us.

"Thank you," he said.

"Yeh," Satta answered and turned toward the way we had come, her certainty unwavering, her life again, if just for a moment, redeemed.

"We go see Mam?" Wi asked.

"Yes," Papa said.

He lifted K to his shoulders and she sat, her hands resting on his head. Wi and I held his hands.

"Come," he said.

We had left everything and run from Caldwell, the pockets of Papa's trousers now emptied, the copper from his change gleaming in the sun. Like the *zokenge* crab that had fought each other to the top of his bucket during those months he fished for food in Lake Piso, now so were his thoughts, it seemed, all climbing. Maybe we were safe and Mam was actually inside that house on the hill; Satta had no reason to lie, and if her plan was to kill us, she would have thrown us into the lake as soon as the canoe left Lai. Papa could have been ambushed in that bus and the rebels could have stolen us. There were the facts—what we had personally experienced and the photograph Satta gave Papa from Mam. But what if Mam was not there? There was so much Papa said he had wanted to tell her while we were hiding, while we were running, but as we walked toward her now he seemed weak. There was love, then there was what he had with Mam; his wildflower, his siren, Orpheus now in the depths, the hell of war, returned for her true loves.

He grunted as we carried on that narrow road up the hill, the breeze and sunset steadfast in their wonder. I would have run if I were not holding Papa's hand. Mam was so close and I was anxious to touch her and tell her of the things she missed.

Papa says he did not know what to expect when the front door of that house creaked its way open. He was hopeful, but he was not certain what we would see.

But there she was.

Mam.

Mam and her beauty, her glorious neck and cheeks, sitting in a chair against the wall, across the front room. She yelled when she saw us. Jallah approached Papa from the couch, but we went straight to Mam.

I ran in to her waiting there, touched her skin as I buried my face in her neck.

"You came back," I said.

She nodded, unable to speak, the familiarity of her eyes jaded by the tears.

After our embrace she went to Papa. They touched each other's faces and backs, they wiped each other's eyes and hugged for a long time, like those days in Caldwell when they stood so close that his arms swallowed her whole. And there was no knowing where she began. And there was no telling where he ended. Then she told us everything. How she prayed for us. Everything that had happened in her America and in the days before we saw her again.

My Ol' Ma says the best stories do not always end happily, but happiness will find its way in there somehow. She says that some will bend many times like the fisher's wire. Some make the children laugh. Some make even the Ol' Pas cry. Some the griots will take a long time to tell, but like plums left in the sun for too long, they too are sweet to taste.

Suffering is a part of everyone's story. As long as my Ol' Ma is here, and I am here, as long as I become an Ol' Ma myself and my children's children become Ol' Mas and Ol' Pas, there will be rainy seasons and dry seasons too long to bear, where troubles pile up like coal to burn you to dust. But just like suffering makes its bed in these seasons, so does happiness, however brief, however fleeting.

There are many stories of war to tell. You will hear them all. But remember among those who were lost, some made it through. Among the dragons there will always be heroes. Even there. Even then. And of those tales ending in defeat, tales of death and orphans wandering among the ruined, some ended the other way too.

Travellers' Pass   January 31, 1991

Officer(s)

    P/s allow the holder(s) of this Pass to travel
to Freetown S/leone on a visit.

Name: Augustus Siaffa Moore

D/D :   Jan. 31, 1991

R/D :   Feb. 14, 1991

ACC.BY: K/ ‗‗‗‗ / Wayetu / K ‗‗‗ (all daughters)

App: ‗‗‗‗‗‗‗‗‗‗‗   signed P. Roberts
    S-2 chief Investigator   J. Jarroe

ACKNOWLEDGMENTS

I want to thank the Moore and Freeman families for your examples of love, compassion, leadership, and integrity. I am grateful, especially, to Gus and Mam Moore who continue to amaze me with their love for each other and for their children. Special thank you to my husband, Eric. Thank you to Agnes Fallah Kamara-Umunna for being an invaluable resource, and to the University of Liberia. To the former child combatants who entrusted me with your stories—thank you for your lesson in forgiveness. Huge thank you to the Community of Writers at Squaw Valley, to Graywolf Press, and to my agent, Susan Golomb. Thank you for Zoe Zolbrod and Martha Bayne for selecting "love/woman/thirty" for publication in the *Sunday Rumpus*. I am grateful to Wiande Everett and Kula Moore-Junge, Susan Henderson, Mary Drummond, Sharon Kim, Eda Henries, and Prentice Onayemi for reading various versions of this book and providing feedback. Thank you to that table of angel girls in the sixth grade who became my sisters and teachers—your magic stays. To the Liberians who read this story as their own: I feel you pushing me along. I thank you. And finally, to Satta. Wherever you are in time—wandering our vast world, in paradise or interstellar—thank you.

WAYÉTU MOORE, author of *She Would Be King*, was born in Liberia and raised in Spring, Texas. She holds a master's degree in creative writing from the University of Southern California and a master's degree in anthropology and education from Columbia University, where she held a Margaret Mead Fellowship. She is a graduate of Howard University and the New York State Summer Writers Institute. Her writing can be found in the *Atlantic*, *Guernica*, and the *Rumpus*, among other publications. She lives in Brooklyn, New York.

The text of *The Dragons, the Giant, the Women*
is set in Adobe Jenson Pro.
Book design by Rachel Holscher.
Composition by Bookmobile Design and Digital
Publisher Services, Minneapolis, Minnesota.
Manufactured by Sheridan on acid-free, 30 percent
postconsumer wastepaper.